Sundays and Solemnities

YEAR

B

PSALMS

FOR THE

LITURGICAL YEAR

The PSALMS *from*
the LECTIONARY *for* CANADA

Sundays and Solemnities

YEAR

B

PSALMS

FOR THE

LITURGICAL YEAR

The PSALMS *from*
the LECTIONARY *for* CANADA

Music by Gordon Johnston

NOVALIS

© 2009 Novalis Publishing Inc.

Psalm settings: © 2009 Gordon Johnston and Novalis
Cover: Ingrid Paulson, Ingrid Paulson Design
Layout: Blair Turner Communication Design Inc.

Published by Novalis

Publishing Office
10 Lower Spadina Avenue, Suite 400
Toronto, Ontario, Canada
M5V 2Z2

Head Office
4475 Frontenac Street
Montréal, Québec, Canada
H2H 2S2

www.novalis.ca

Library and Archives Canada Cataloguing in Publication

ISBN 978-2-89646-081-6

Printed in Canada.

We acknowledge the support of the Government of Canada.

6   5   4   3   2   21   20   19   18   17

Table of Contents

Solemnities of the Lord during Ordinary Time

Ordinary Time

Feasts and Solemnities Replacing Sundays

Table of Responsorial Psalms and Canticles

Table of Psalm Refrains

Introduction

These psalm settings are intended to be sung by a solo cantor, with the response sung by the choir and congregation. Accompaniment parts are given for keyboard, guitar, C instrument (flute, oboe, recorder, etc.) and B-flat instrument (trumpet, clarinet, etc.). The instrumental lines are meant to accompany the refrain. Instruments may also be used to double the melody line of the refrain.

A unique characteristic of this music is the "bridge" which connects the cantor's verse to the congregational refrain. The fermata ⌢ over the final note of the refrain is intended to show the end of the phrase, not to indicate that the music should slow down or hold on that note. The symbol *D.C. (da capo)* at the end of the second line of music indicates that the accompaniment returns to the beginning without stopping.

How the psalms are sung

These psalms should be performed in the following manner:

- As an introduction, play the refrain through, stopping at the fermata.

- The cantor sings the refrain. This time, the accompaniment doesn't stop at the fermata, but continues on, playing the bridge, and then repeats the refrain for the congregation to sing, this time stopping at the fermata.

- Now the cantor sings the first verse. On the last note of the psalm tone, the tempo is re-established; play the bridge in tempo, returning to the refrain for everyone to sing, stopping at the fermata.

- Subsequent verses continue this pattern, so there is a break between the congregational refrain and the new verse by the cantor, but a smooth transition from the cantor back to the congregation.

The purpose of the musical bridge which connects the cantor's verse to the congregation's refrain is to indicate the tempo and pitch of the refrain for the congregation so that they can sing their part with confidence. In order for them to do that, it's important that the accompanist **not slow down** just before they begin singing; the purpose is to lead the congregation into their part, so a steady, reliable tempo is essential.

How the psalms are pointed

The psalm tones in this collection have been written to match the lines of the psalm. Each line is pointed using a bullet and bold print to indicate when to move. You move on the bold word. For example, if the music has a reciting tone and one note following, the text would be pointed:

> I will bless the Lord at all · **times.**

If two words are to be sung to one note, they are joined together with an underscore:

> With my whole heart **I** · **seek_you.**

If a word of several syllables is to be divided over more than one note, the hyphen shows the division:

> Let me not stray from your com·-**mandments.**

Most psalm texts are divided into groups of four lines each. The accompanying psalm tone will have four measures, one for each line. In a few rare instances, one verse will have fewer lines than the other verses. In that case, the number of the measure precedes the text. For example,

> 1 – Be glad in the Lord and rejoice, O · **righteous,**
> 4 – and shout for joy, all you upright in · **heart.**

In this case, you would sing the first line to the first measure of the psalm tone, then omit measures 2 and 3, and sing the second line to measure 4, continuing on to the bridge and the refrain.

The singing of the psalms should be like musical speech, free and natural, never measured or forced. The note values of the refrain are exact, but the verses are meant to be sung and played in free time, following the natural flow of the text.

A few general thoughts

It is always important to teach the people the psalm refrain before the celebration begins, unless it is a seasonal refrain that is well known. Play the refrain on the keyboard, if you're using one, then sing the refrain and invite the congregation to sing it back.

Music ministers and cantors should always learn the psalm well before the liturgy so they can lead the assembly in singing the refrain, and enable the assembly to meditate on the Word as the cantor sings the verses. Respect for Christ's presence in the Word and in the worshipping assembly should motivate us to prepare and give only our best.

If you would like to hear how a particular psalm goes, go to
http://www.livingwithchrist.ca/index.php/psalms-year

Sundays and Solemnities

YEAR

B

Common Psalm for Advent

Psalm 25

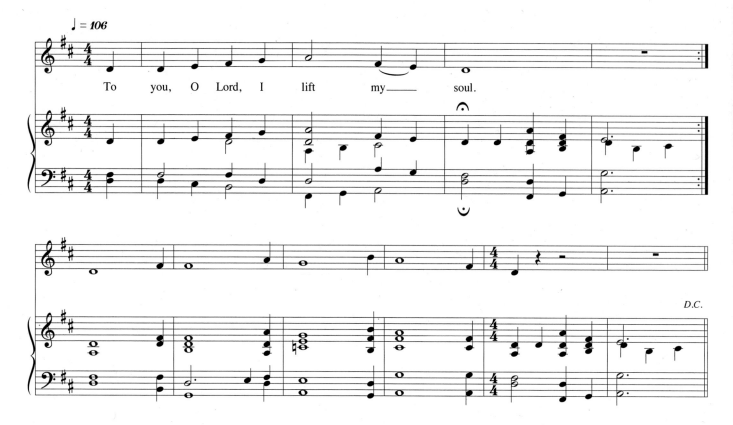

To you, O Lord, I lift my soul.

Make me to know your ways, O · **Lord,**
teach me your · **paths.**
Lead me in your truth and · **teach_me,**
for you are the God of my · **sal**-vation. R.

Good and upright is the · **Lord,**
therefore he instructs sinners in the · **way.**
He leads the humble in what is · **right,**
and teaches the humble · **his** way. R.

All the paths of the Lord are steadfast love and · **faithfulness,**
for those who keep his covenant and his de·-**crees.**
The friendship of the Lord is for those who · **fear_him,**
and he makes his covenant known · **to** them. R.

Common Psalm for Advent

Psalm 25

To you, O Lord, I lift my—— soul.

Make me to know your ways, O · **Lord,**
teach me your · **paths.**
Lead me in your truth and · **teach_me,**
for you are the God of my · **sal**-vation. R.

Good and upright is the · **Lord,**
therefore he instructs sinners in the · **way.**
He leads the humble in what is · **right,**
and teaches the humble · **his** way. R.

All the paths of the Lord are steadfast love and · **faithfulness,**
for those who keep his covenant and his de-·**crees.**
The friendship of the Lord is for those who · **fear_him,**
and he makes his covenant known · **to** them. R.

C Instrument

B♭ Instrument

3

Common Psalm for Advent

Psalm 85

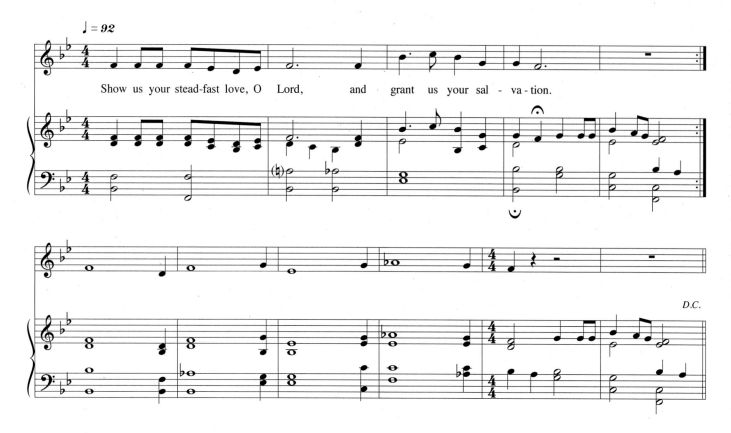

Show us your stead-fast love, O Lord, and grant us your sal - va - tion.

Let me hear what God the Lord will · **speak,**
for he will speak peace to his · **people.**
Surely his salvation is at hand for those who · **fear_him,**
that his glory may dwell · **in_our** land. R.

Steadfast love and faithfulness will · **meet;**
righteousness and peace will · **kiss_each_other.**
Faithfulness will spring up from the · **ground,**
and righteousness will look down · **from_the** sky. R.

The Lord will give what is · **good,**
and our land will yield its · **increase.**
Righteousness will go be·-**fore_him,**
and will make a path · **for_his** steps. R.

Common Psalm for Advent

Psalm 85

Guitar

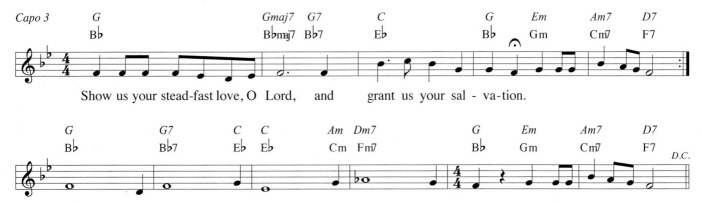

Show us your stead-fast love, O Lord, and grant us your sal - va-tion.

Let me hear what God the Lord will · **speak,**
for he will speak peace to his · **people.**
Surely his salvation is at hand for those who · **fear_him,**
that his glory may dwell · **in_our** land. R.

Steadfast love and faithfulness will · **meet;**
righteousness and peace will · **kiss_each_other.**
Faithfulness will spring up from the · **ground,**
and righteousness will look down · **from_the** sky. R.

The Lord will give what is · **good,**
and our land will yield its · **increase.**
Righteousness will go be·-**fore_him,**
and will make a path · **for_his** steps. R.

C Instrument

B♭ Instrument

Common Psalm for Advent

Psalm 146

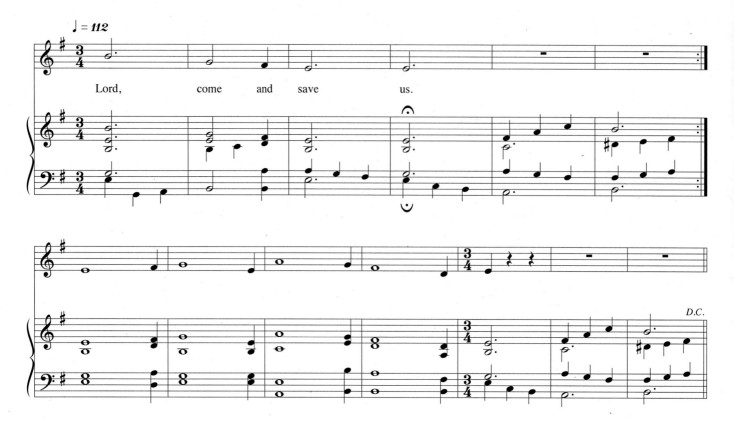

Lord, come and save us.

It is the Lord who keeps faith for·-**ever,**
who executes justice for the op·-**pressed;**
who gives food to the · **hungry.**
The Lord sets the · **prisoners** free. R.

The Lord opens the eyes of the · **blind**
and lifts up those who are bowed · **down;**
the Lord loves the · **righteous**
and watches over · **the** strangers. R.

The Lord upholds the orphan and the · **widow,**
but the way of the wicked he brings to · **ruin.**
The Lord will reign for·-**ever,**
your God, O Zion, for all · **gener**-ations. R.

6

Common Psalm for Advent
Psalm 146

Guitar

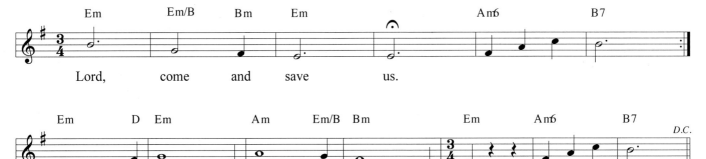

Lord, come and save us.

It is the Lord who keeps faith for·-**ever,**
who executes justice for the op·-**pressed;**
who gives food to the · **hungry.**
The Lord sets the · **prisoners** free. R.

The Lord opens the eyes of the · **blind**
and lifts up those who are bowed · **down;**
the Lord loves the · **righteous**
and watches over · **the** strangers. R.

The Lord upholds the orphan and the · **widow,**
but the way of the wicked he brings to · **ruin.**
The Lord will reign for·-**ever,**
your God, O Zion, for all · **gener**-ations. R.

C Instrument

B♭ Instrument

7

First Sunday of Advent – B

Psalm 80

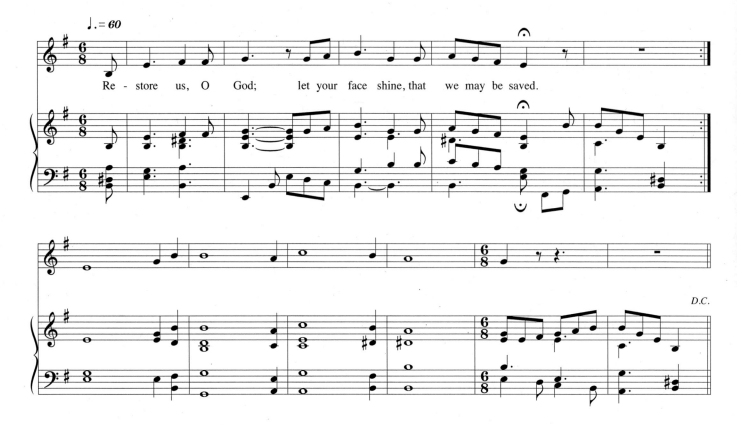

Re - store us, O God; let your face shine, that we may be saved.

Give ear, O Shepherd · **of** Israel,
you who are enthroned upon the cherubim, shine · **forth.**
Stir up your · **might,**
and come to · **save_us.** R.

Turn again, O God · **of** hosts;
look down from heaven, and · **see;**
have regard for this · **vine,**
the stock that your right hand has · **planted.** R.

But let your hand be upon the man at · **your** right,
the son of man you have made strong for your·-**self.**
Then we will never turn · **back_from_you;**
give us life, and we will call on your · **name.** R.

First Sunday of Advent – B

Psalm 80

Guitar

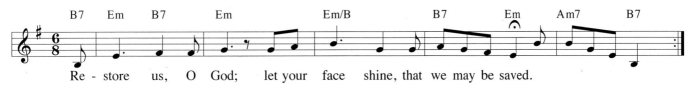

Re - store us, O God; let your face shine, that we may be saved.

Give ear, O Shepherd · **of** Israel,
you who are enthroned upon the cherubim, shine · **forth.**
Stir up your · **might,**
and come to · **save_us.** R.

Turn again, O God · **of** hosts;
look down from heaven, and · **see;**
have regard for this · **vine,**
the stock that your right hand has · **planted.** R.

But let your hand be upon the man at · **your** right,
the son of man you have made strong for your·-**self.**
Then we will never turn · **back_from_you;**
give us life, and we will call on your · **name.** R.

C Instrument

B♭ Instrument

Second Sunday of Advent – B

Psalm 85

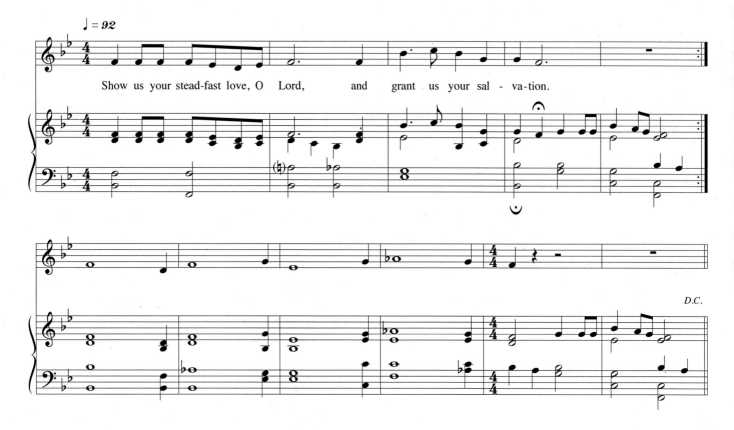

Show us your stead-fast love, O Lord, and grant us your sal - va-tion.

Let me hear what God the Lord will · **speak,**
for he will speak peace to his · **people.**
Surely his salvation is at hand for those who · **fear_him,**
that his glory may dwell · **in_our** land. R.

Steadfast love and faithfulness will · **meet;**
righteousness and peace will · **kiss_each_other.**
Faithfulness will spring up from the · **ground,**
and righteousness will look down · **from_the** sky. R.

The Lord will give what is · **good,**
and our land will yield its · **increase.**
Righteousness will go be·-**fore_him,**
and will make a path · **for_his** steps. R.

Second Sunday of Advent – B

Psalm 85

Guitar

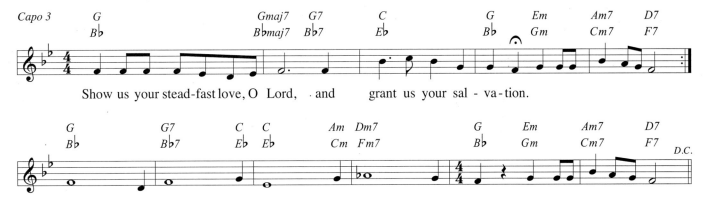

Show us your stead-fast love, O Lord, and grant us your sal - va - tion.

Let me hear what God the Lord will · **speak,**
for he will speak peace to his · **people.**
Surely his salvation is at hand for those who · **fear_him,**
that his glory may dwell · **in_our** land. R.

Steadfast love and faithfulness will · **meet;**
righteousness and peace will · **kiss_each_other.**
Faithfulness will spring up from the · **ground,**
and righteousness will look down · **from_the** sky. R.

The Lord will give what is · **good,**
and our land will yield its · **increase.**
Righteousness will go be·-**fore_him,**
and will make a path · **for_his** steps. R.

C Instrument

B♭ Instrument

Third Sunday of Advent – B

Luke 1

My soul shall ex-ult in my God.

D.C.

My soul magnifies the · **Lord**
and my spirit rejoices in God · **my** Saviour,
for he has looked with favour on the lowliness of his · **servant.**
Surely, from now on all generations will · **call_me** blessed. R.

For the Mighty One has done great things for · **me,**
and holy is · **his** name.
His mercy is for those who · **fear_him**
from generation to · **gener**-ation. R.

The Lord has filled the hungry with · **good_things**
and sent the rich a·-**way** empty.
He has helped his servant · **Israel,**
in remembrance · **of_his** mercy. R.

Third Sunday of Advent – B

Luke 1

Guitar

My soul shall ex - ult in my God.

My soul magnifies the · **Lord**
and my spirit rejoices in God · **my** Saviour,
for he has looked with favour on the lowliness of his · **servant.**
Surely, from now on all generations will · **call_me** blessed. R.

For the Mighty One has done great things for · **me,**
and holy is · **his** name.
His mercy is for those who · **fear_him**
from generation to · **gener**-ation. R.

The Lord has filled the hungry with · **good_things**
and sent the rich a-·**way** empty.
He has helped his servant · **Israel,**
in remembrance · **of_his** mercy. R.

C Instrument

B♭ Instrument

Fourth Sunday of Advent – B

Psalm 89

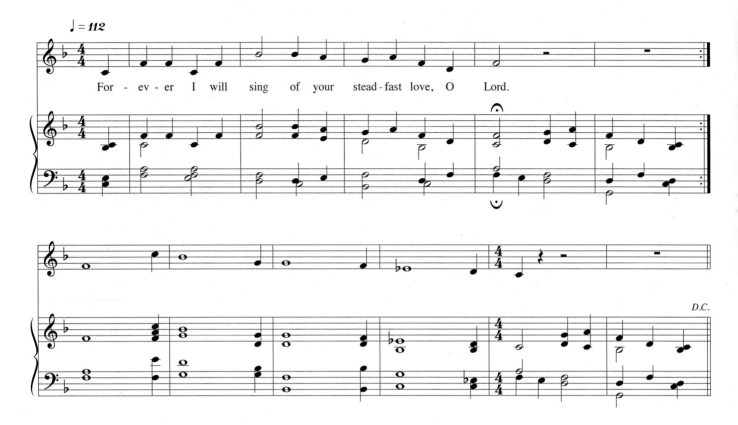

I will sing of your steadfast love, O Lord, for·-**ever;**
with my mouth I will proclaim your faithfulness to all gener·-**ations.**
I declare that your steadfast love is established for·-**ever;**
your faithfulness is as firm · **as_the** heavens. R.

You said, "I have made a covenant with my · **chosen_one,**
I have sworn to my servant · **David:**
I will establish your descendants for·-**ever,**
and build your throne for all · **gener**-ations." R.

He shall cry to me, "You are my · **Father,**
my God, and the Rock of my sal·-**vation!"**
Forever I will keep my steadfast · **love_for_him,**
and my covenant with him will · **stand** firm. R.

Fourth Sunday of Advent – B

Psalm 89

Guitar

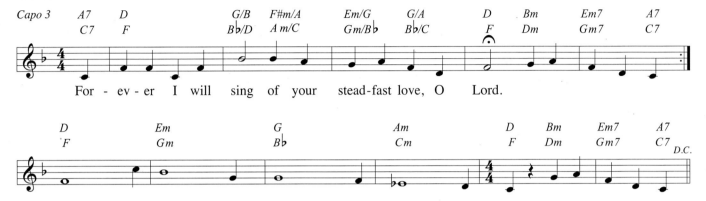

For - ev - er I will sing of your stead-fast love, O Lord.

I will sing of your steadfast love, O Lord, for·-**ever;**
with my mouth I will proclaim your faithfulness to all gener·-**ations.**
I declare that your steadfast love is established for·-**ever;**
your faithfulness is as firm · **as_the** heavens. R.

You said, "I have made a covenant with my · **chosen_one,**
I have sworn to my servant · **David:**
I will establish your descendants for·-**ever,**
and build your throne for all · **gener**-ations." R.

He shall cry to me, "You are my · **Father,**
my God, and the Rock of my sal·-**vation!**"
Forever I will keep my steadfast · **love_for_him,**
and my covenant with him will · **stand** firm. R.

C Instrument

B♭ Instrument

Common Psalm for Christmas

Psalm 98

O sing to the Lord a · **new** song,
for he has done · **marvellous** things.
His right hand and his holy · **arm**
have brought · **him** victory. R.

The Lord has made known · **his** victory;
he has revealed his vindication in the sight of · **the** nations.
He has remembered his steadfast love and · **faithfulness**
to the house · **of** Israel. R.

All the ends of the earth · **have** seen
the victory of · **our** God.
Make a joyful noise to the Lord, all the · **earth;**
break forth into joyous song and · **sing** praises. R.

Sing praises to the Lord with · **the** lyre,
with the lyre and the sound · **of** melody.
With trumpets and the sound of the · **horn**
make a joyful noise before the King, · **the** Lord. R.

Common Psalm for Christmas
Psalm 98

Guitar

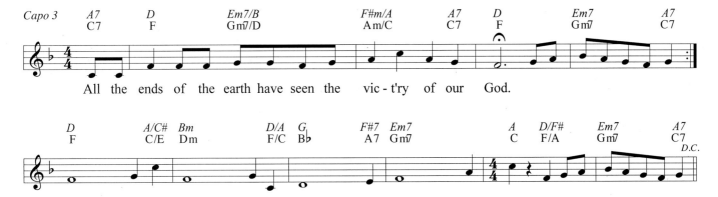

All the ends of the earth have seen the vic-t'ry of our God.

O sing to the Lord a · **new** song,
for he has done · **marvellous** things.
His right hand and his holy · **arm**
have brought · **him** victory. R.

The Lord has made known · **his** victory;
he has revealed his vindication in the sight of · **the** nations.
He has remembered his steadfast love and · **faithfulness**
to the house · **of** Israel. R.

All the ends of the earth · **have** seen
the victory of · **our** God.
Make a joyful noise to the Lord, all the · **earth;**
break forth into joyous song and · **sing** praises. R.

Sing praises to the Lord with · **the** lyre,
with the lyre and the sound · **of** melody.
With trumpets and the sound of the · **horn**
make a joyful noise before the King, · **the** Lord. R.

C Instrument

B♭ Instrument

Common Psalm for Christmas
Psalm 34

I will bless the Lord at all · **times;**
his praise shall continually be in · **my** mouth.
My soul makes its boast in the · **Lord;**
let the humble hear and · **be** glad. R.

O fear the Lord, you his · **holy_ones,**
for those who fear him have · **no** want.
The young lions suffer want and · **hunger,**
but those who seek the Lord lack no · **good** thing. R.

Come, O children, · **listen_to_me;**
I will teach you the fear of · **the** Lord.
Which of you desires · **life,**
and covets many days to en-·**joy** good? R.

Keep your tongue from · **evil,**
and your lips from speaking · **de-**ceit.
Depart from evil, and do · **good;**
seek peace, and · **pur-**sue_it. R.

Common Psalm for Christmas

Psalm 34

Guitar

Bless - ed the one who fears the Lord.

I will bless the Lord at all · **times;**
his praise shall continually be in · **my** mouth.
My soul makes its boast in the · **Lord;**
let the humble hear and · **be** glad. R.

O fear the Lord, you his · **holy_ones,**
for those who fear him have · **no** want.
The young lions suffer want and · **hunger,**
but those who seek the Lord lack no · **good** thing. R.

Come, O children, · **listen_to_me;**
I will teach you the fear of · **the** Lord.
Which of you desires · **life,**
and covets many days to en·-**joy** good? R.

Keep your tongue from · **evil,**
and your lips from speaking · **de**-ceit.
Depart from evil, and do · **good;**
seek peace, and · **pur**-sue_it. R.

C Instrument

B♭ Instrument

Common Psalm for Christmas

Psalm 72

Give the king your justice, O · **God,**
and your righteousness to a king's · **son.**
May he judge your · **people** with righteousness,
and your · **poor** with justice. R.

In his days may righteousness · **flourish**
and peace abound, until the moon is no · **more.**
May he have dominion from · **sea** to sea,
and from the River to the · **ends_of** the earth. R.

May the kings of Tarshish and of the isles render him · **tribute,**
may the kings of Sheba and Seba bring · **gifts.**
May all kings fall · **down** be-fore_him,
all nations · **give** him service. R.

For he delivers the needy one who · **calls,**
the poor and the one who has no · **helper.**
He has pity on the · **weak_and** the needy,
and saves the · **lives_of** the needy. R.

Common Psalm for Christmas

Psalm 72

Guitar

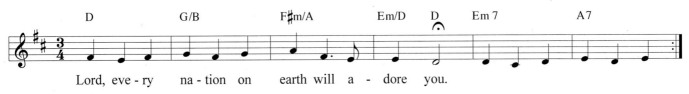

Lord, eve - ry na - tion on earth will a - dore you.

Give the king your justice, O · **God,**
and your righteousness to a king's · **son.**
May he judge your · **people** with righteousness,
and your · **poor** with justice. R.

In his days may righteousness · **flourish**
and peace abound, until the moon is no · **more.**
May he have dominion from · **sea** to sea,
and from the River to the · **ends_of** the earth. R.

May the kings of Tarshish and of the isles render him · **tribute,**
may the kings of Sheba and Seba bring · **gifts.**
May all kings fall · **down** be-fore_him,
all nations · **give** him service. R.

For he delivers the needy one who · **calls,**
the poor and the one who has no · **helper.**
He has pity on the · **weak_and** the needy,
and saves the · **lives_of** the needy. R.

C Instrument

B♭ Instrument

Christmas: Nativity of the Lord (Vigil) – ABC

Psalm 89

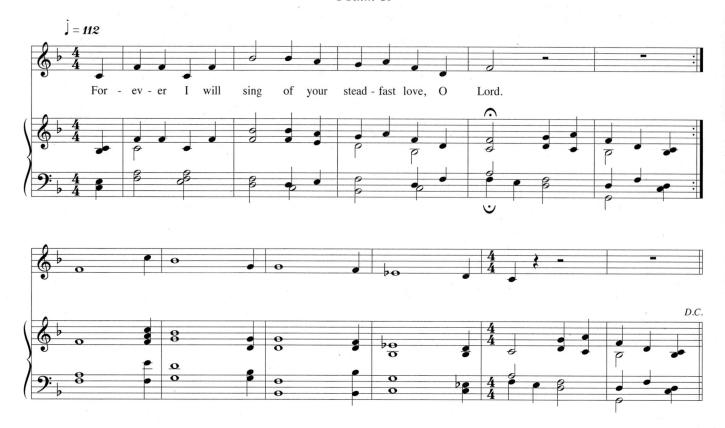

Forever I will sing of your steadfast love, O Lord.

D.C.

You said, "I have made a covenant with my · **chosen_one,**
I have sworn to my servant · **David:**
I will establish your descendants for·-**ever,**
and build your throne for all · **gener**-ations." R.

Blessed are the people who know the festal · **shout,**
who walk, O Lord, in the light of your · **countenance;**
they exult in your name all day · **long,**
and extol · **your** righteousness. R.

He shall cry to me, "You are my · **Father,**
my God, and the Rock of my sal·-**vation!**"
Forever I will keep my steadfast love for · **him,**
and my covenant with him will · **stand** firm. R.

Christmas: Nativity of the Lord (Vigil) – ABC

Psalm 89

Guitar

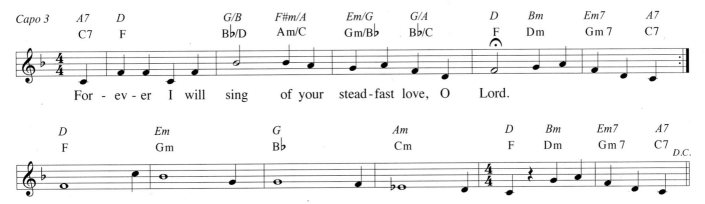

Lyrics under the melody: For - ev - er I will sing of your stead-fast love, O Lord.

You said, "I have made a covenant with my · **chosen_one,**
I have sworn to my servant · **David:**
I will establish your descendants for·-**ever,**
and build your throne for all · **gener**-ations." R.

Blessed are the people who know the festal · **shout,**
who walk, O Lord, in the light of your · **countenance;**
they exult in your name all day · **long,**
and extol · **your** righteousness. R.

He shall cry to me, "You are my · **Father,**
my God, and the Rock of my sal·-**vation!**"
Forever I will keep my steadfast love for · **him,**
and my covenant with him will · **stand** firm. R.

C Instrument

B♭ Instrument

Christmas: Nativity of the Lord (Night) – ABC

Psalm 96

Today is born our Saviour,—— Christ—— the Lord.

D.C.

O sing to the Lord a · **new** song;
sing to the Lord, · **all_the** earth.
Sing to the Lord, · **bless_his** name;
tell of his salvation from day · **to** day. R.

Declare his glory among · **the** nations,
his marvellous works among all · **the** peoples.
For great is the Lord, and greatly · **to_be** praised;
he is to be revered above · **all** gods. R.

Let the heavens be glad, and let the earth · **re**-joice;
let the sea roar, and all · **that** fills_it;
let the field exult, and every·-**thing** in_it.
Then shall all the trees of the forest sing · **for** joy. R.

Rejoice before the Lord; for · **he_is** coming,
for he is coming to judge · **the** earth.
He will judge the world · **with** righteousness,
and the peoples · **with_his** truth. R.

Christmas: Nativity of the Lord (Night) – ABC

Psalm 96

Guitar

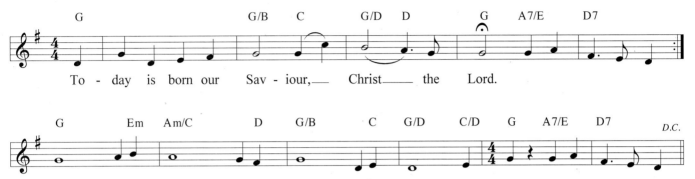

To - day is born our Sav - iour,___ Christ___ the Lord.

O sing to the Lord a · **new** song;
sing to the Lord, · **all_the** earth.
Sing to the Lord, · **bless_his** name;
tell of his salvation from day · **to** day. R.

Declare his glory among · **the** nations,
his marvellous works among all · **the** peoples.
For great is the Lord, and greatly · **to_be** praised;
he is to be revered above · **all** gods. R.

Let the heavens be glad, and let the earth · **re**-joice;
let the sea roar, and all · **that** fills_it;
let the field exult, and every·-**thing** in_it.
Then shall all the trees of the forest sing · **for** joy. R.

Rejoice before the Lord; for · **he_is** coming,
for he is coming to judge · **the** earth.
He will judge the world · **with** righteousness,
and the peoples · **with_his** truth. R.

C Instrument

B♭ Instrument

Christmas: Nativity of the Lord (Dawn) – ABC

Psalm 97

A light will shine on us this day: the Lord is born for us.

The Lord is king! Let the earth re·-**joice;**
let the many coastlands be · **glad!**
Clouds and thick darkness are all a·-**round_him;**
righteousness and justice are the foundation of his · **throne.** R.

The mountains melt like wax before the · **Lord,**
before the Lord of all the · **earth.**
The heavens proclaim his · **righteousness;**
and all the peoples behold his · **glory.** R.

Light dawns for the · **righteous,**
and joy for the upright in · **heart.**
Rejoice in the Lord, O you · **righteous,**
and give thanks to his holy · **name!** R.

Christmas: Nativity of the Lord (Dawn) – ABC

Psalm 97

Guitar

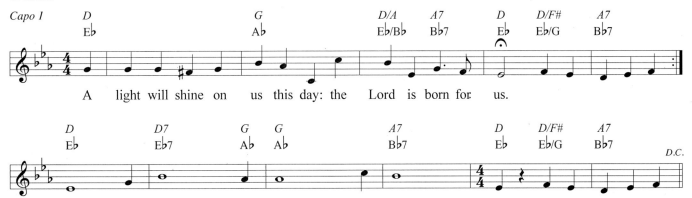

The Lord is king! Let the earth re-·**joice;**
let the many coastlands be · **glad!**
Clouds and thick darkness are all a-·**round_him;**
righteousness and justice are the foundation of his · **throne.** R.

The mountains melt like wax before the · **Lord,**
before the Lord of all the · **earth.**
The heavens proclaim his · **righteousness;**
and all the peoples behold his · **glory.** R.

Light dawns for the · **righteous,**
and joy for the upright in · **heart.**
Rejoice in the Lord, O you · **righteous,**
and give thanks to his holy · **name!** R.

C Instrument

B♭ Instrument

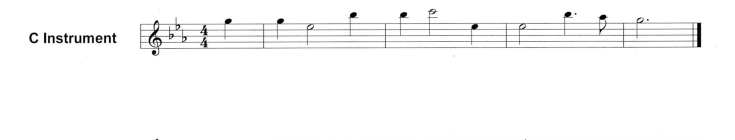

Christmas: Nativity of the Lord (Day) – ABC

Psalm 98

All the ends of the earth have seen the vic-t'ry of our God.

O sing to the Lord a · **new** song,
for he has done · **marvellous** things.
His right hand and his holy · **arm**
have brought · **him** victory. R.

The Lord has made known · **his** victory;
he has revealed his vindication in the sight of · **the** nations.
He has remembered his steadfast love and · **faithfulness**
to the house · **of** Israel. R.

All the ends of the earth · **have** seen
the victory of · **our** God.
Make a joyful noise to the Lord, all the · **earth;**
break forth into joyous song and · **sing** praises. R.

Sing praises to the Lord with · **the** lyre,
with the lyre and the sound · **of** melody.
With trumpets and the sound of the · **horn**
make a joyful noise before the King, · **the** Lord. R.

Christmas: Nativity of the Lord (Day) – ABC

Psalm 98

Guitar

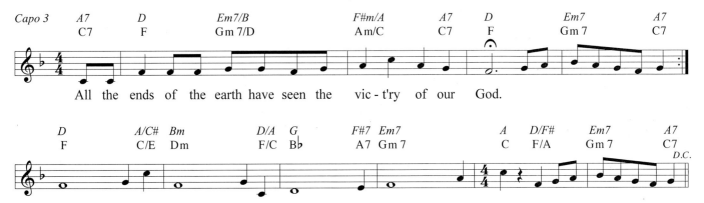

All the ends of the earth have seen the vic-t'ry of our God.

O sing to the Lord a · **new** song,
for he has done · **marvellous** things.
His right hand and his holy · **arm**
have brought · **him** victory. R.

The Lord has made known · **his** victory;
he has revealed his vindication in the sight of · **the** nations.
He has remembered his steadfast love and · **faithfulness**
to the house · **of** Israel. R.

All the ends of the earth · **have** seen
the victory of · **our** God.
Make a joyful noise to the Lord, all the · **earth;**
break forth into joyous song and · **sing** praises. R.

Sing praises to the Lord with · **the** lyre,
with the lyre and the sound · **of** melody.
With trumpets and the sound of the · **horn**
make a joyful noise before the King, · **the** Lord. R.

C Instrument

B♭ Instrument

Holy Family of Jesus, Mary and Joseph – B

Psalm 105

The Lord is our God, mind-ful___ of his cov-e-nant for-ev-er.

O give thanks to the Lord, call · **on_his** name,
make known his deeds a·-**mong_the** peoples.
Sing to him, sing · **praises** to him;
tell of all his · **wonderful** works. R.

Glory in his ho·-**ly** name;
let the hearts of those who seek the Lord · **re**-joice.
Seek the Lord · **and** his strength;
seek his presence · **con**-tinually. R.

Remember the wonderful works he · **has** done,
his miracles, and the judgments · **he** uttered,
O offspring of his · **ser**-vant Abraham,
children of Jacob, · **his** chosen_ones. R.

He is mindful of his covenant · **for**-ever,
of the word that he commanded, for a thousand · **gener**-ations,
the covenant that he · **made** with Abraham,
his sworn promise · **to** Isaac. R.

Holy Family of Jesus, Mary and Joseph – B

Psalm 105

Guitar

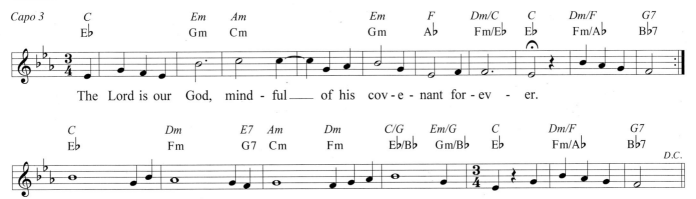

The Lord is our God, mind - ful ___ of his cov - e - nant for - ev - er.

O give thanks to the Lord, call · **on_his** name,
make known his deeds a·-**mong_the** peoples.
Sing to him, sing · **praises** to him;
tell of all his · **wonderful** works. R.

Glory in his ho·-**ly** name;
let the hearts of those who seek the Lord · **re**-joice.
Seek the Lord · **and** his strength;
seek his presence · **con**-tinually. R.

Remember the wonderful works he · **has** done,
his miracles, and the judgments · **he** uttered,
O offspring of his · **ser**-vant Abraham,
children of Jacob, · **his** chosen_ones. R.

He is mindful of his covenant · **for**-ever,
of the word that he commanded, for a thousand · **gener**-ations,
the covenant that he · **made** with Abraham,
his sworn promise · **to** Isaac. R.

C Instrument

B♭ Instrument

Holy Family of Jesus, Mary and Joseph – ABC

Psalm 128

Bless-ed is eve-ry-one who fears the Lord, who walks in his ways.

Blessed is everyone who fears · **the** Lord,
who walks in · **his** ways.
You shall eat the fruit of the labour of · **your** hands;
you shall be happy, and it shall go well · **with** you. R.

Your wife will be like a fruit·-**ful** vine
within · **your** house;
your children will be · **like** olive_shoots
around · **your** table. R.

Thus shall the man be blessed who fears · **the** Lord.
The Lord bless you · **from** Zion.
May you see the prosperity of · **Je**-rusalem
all the days of · **your** life. R.

Holy Family of Jesus, Mary and Joseph – ABC

Psalm 128

Guitar

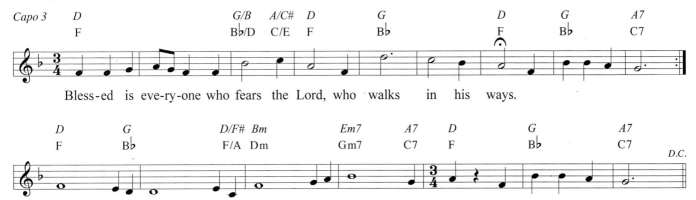

Bless-ed is eve-ry-one who fears the Lord, who walks in his ways.

Blessed is everyone who fears · **the** Lord,
who walks in · **his** ways.
You shall eat the fruit of the labour of · **your** hands;
you shall be happy, and it shall go well · **with** you. R.

Your wife will be like a fruit·-**ful** vine
within · **your** house;
your children will be · **like** olive_shoots
around · **your** table. R.

Thus shall the man be blessed who fears · **the** Lord.
The Lord bless you · **from** Zion.
May you see the prosperity of · **Je**-rusalem
all the days of · **your** life. R.

C Instrument

B♭ Instrument

33

January 1 – Solemnity of Mary, the Holy Mother of God – ABC

Psalm 67

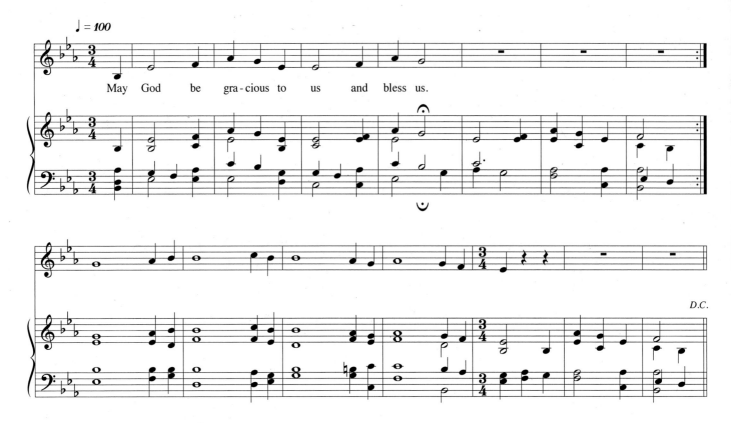

May God be gracious to us · **and** bless_us
and make his face to shine · **up**-on_us,
that your way may be known up·-**on** earth,
your saving power a·-**mong** all nations. R.

Let the nations be glad and sing · **for** joy,
for you judge the peoples with equity and guide the nations up·-**on** earth.
Let the peoples praise you, · **O** God;
let all the · **peo**-ples praise_you. R.

The earth has yielded · **its** increase;
God, our God, · **has** blessed_us.
May God continue · **to** bless_us;
let all the ends of the · **earth** re-vere_him. R.

January 1 – Solemnity of Mary, the Holy Mother of God – ABC

Psalm 67

Guitar

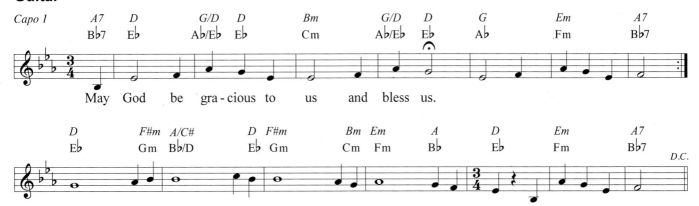

May God be gracious to us and bless us.

May God be gracious to us · **and** bless_us
and make his face to shine · **up**-on_us,
that your way may be known up·-**on** earth,
your saving power a·-**mong** all nations. R.

Let the nations be glad and sing · **for** joy,
for you judge the peoples with equity and guide the nations up·-**on** earth.
Let the peoples praise you, · **O** God;
let all the · **peo**-ples praise_you. R.

The earth has yielded · **its** increase;
God, our God, · **has** blessed_us.
May God continue · **to** bless_us;
let all the ends of the · **earth** re-vere_him. R.

C Instrument

B♭ Instrument

Second Sunday after Christmas – ABC

Psalm 147

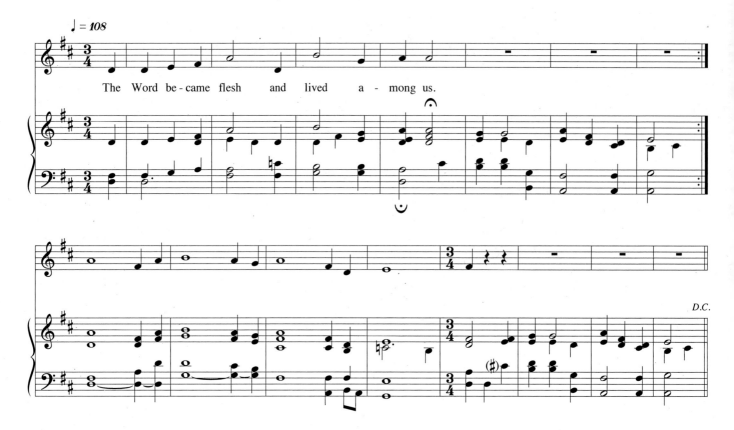

The Word be-came flesh and lived a - mong us.

D.C.

Praise the Lord, O · **Je**-rusalem!
Praise your God, · **O** Zion!
For he strengthens the bars of · **your** gates;
he blesses your children with·-**in_you.** R.

He grants peace within · **your** borders;
he fills you with the finest · **of** wheat.
He sends out his command · **to_the** earth;
his word runs · **swiftly.** R.

He declares his word · **to** Jacob,
his statutes and ordinances · **to** Israel.
He has not dealt thus with any · **other** nation;
they do not know his · **ordinances.** R.

Second Sunday after Christmas – ABC

Psalm 147

Guitar

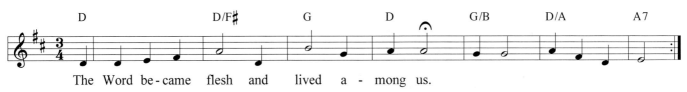

The Word be-came flesh and lived a - mong us.

Praise the Lord, O · **Je**-rusalem!
Praise your God, · **O** Zion!
For he strengthens the bars of · **your** gates;
he blesses your children with·-**in_you.** R.

He grants peace within · **your** borders;
he fills you with the finest · **of** wheat.
He sends out his command · **to_the** earth;
his word runs · **swiftly.** R.

He declares his word · **to** Jacob,
his statutes and ordinances · **to** Israel.
He has not dealt thus with any · **other** nation;
they do not know his · **ordinances.** R.

C Instrument

B♭ Instrument

Epiphany of the Lord – ABC

Psalm 72

Lord, eve-ry na-tion on earth will a-dore you.

Give the king your justice, O · **God,**
and your righteousness to a king's · **son.**
May he judge your · **people** with righteousness,
and your · **poor** with justice. R.

In his days may righteousness · **flourish**
and peace abound, until the moon is no · **more.**
May he have dominion from · **sea** to sea,
and from the River to the · **ends_of** the earth. R.

May the kings of Tarshish and of the isles render him · **tribute,**
may the kings of Sheba and Seba bring · **gifts.**
May all kings fall · **down** be-fore_him,
all nations · **give** him service. R.

For he delivers the needy one who · **calls,**
the poor and the one who has no · **helper.**
He has pity on the · **weak_and** the needy,
and saves the · **lives_of** the needy. R.

Epiphany of the Lord – ABC

Psalm 72

Guitar

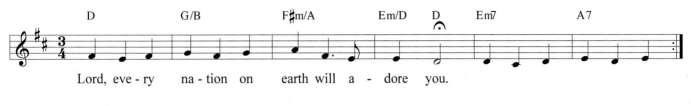

Lord, eve-ry na-tion on earth will a - dore you.

Give the king your justice, O · **God,**
and your righteousness to a king's · **son.**
May he judge your · **people** with righteousness,
and your · **poor** with justice. R.

In his days may righteousness · **flourish**
and peace abound, until the moon is no · **more.**
May he have dominion from · **sea** to sea,
and from the River to the · **ends_of** the earth. R.

May the kings of Tarshish and of the isles render him · **tribute,**
may the kings of Sheba and Seba bring · **gifts.**
May all kings fall · **down** be-fore_him,
all nations · **give** him service. R.

For he delivers the needy one who · **calls,**
the poor and the one who has no · **helper.**
He has pity on the · **weak_and** the needy,
and saves the · **lives_of** the needy. R.

C Instrument

B♭ Instrument

Baptism of the Lord – B

Isaiah 12

With joy you will draw wa-ter ___ from the wells of sal - va-tion.

Surely God is my salvation; I will trust, and will not · **be** a-fraid,
for the Lord God is my strength and my might; he has be·-**come_my** sal-vation.
With joy · **you_will** draw water
from the wells · **of** sal-vation. R.

Give thanks · **to** the Lord,
call · **on** his name;
make known his deeds a·-**mong** the nations;
proclaim that his · **name_is** ex-alted. R.

Sing praises to the Lord, for he · **has** done gloriously;
let this be known in · **all** the earth.
Shout aloud and sing for joy, O · **roy**-al Zion,
for great in your midst is the Holy · **One** of Israel. R.

Baptism of the Lord – B

Isaiah 12

Guitar

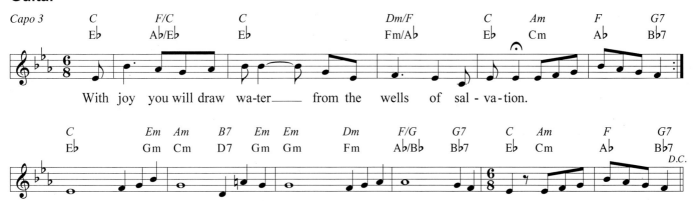

With joy you will draw wa-ter___ from the wells of sal-va-tion.

Surely God is my salvation; I will trust, and will not · **be** a-fraid,
for the Lord God is my strength and my might; he has be·-**come_my** sal-vation.
With joy · **you_will** draw water
from the wells · **of** sal-vation. R.

Give thanks · **to** the Lord,
call · **on** his name;
make known his deeds a·-**mong** the nations;
proclaim that his · **name_is** ex-alted. R.

Sing praises to the Lord, for he · **has** done gloriously;
let this be known in · **all** the earth.
Shout aloud and sing for joy, O · **roy**-al Zion,
for great in your midst is the Holy · **One** of Israel. R.

C Instrument

B♭ Instrument

Baptism of the Lord – ABC

Psalm 29

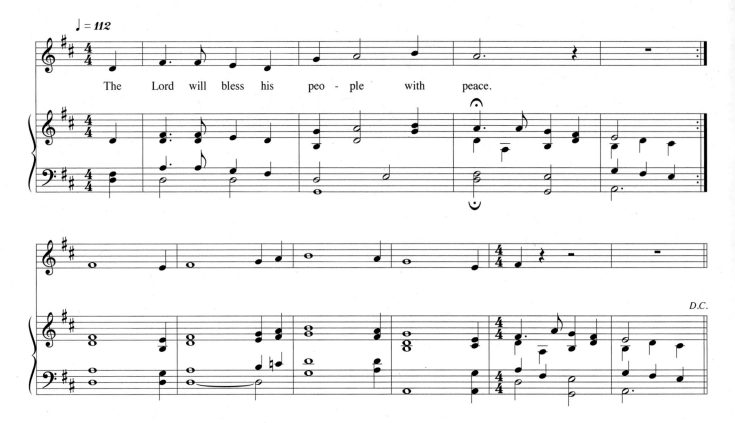

The Lord will bless his peo-ple with peace.

Ascribe to the Lord, O heavenly · **beings,**
ascribe to the Lord glory · **and** strength.
Ascribe to the Lord the glory of his · **name;**
worship the Lord in · **holy** splendour. R.

The voice of the Lord is over the · **waters;**
the Lord, over · **mighty** waters.
The voice of the Lord is · **powerful;**
the voice of the Lord is · **full_of** majesty. R.

The God of glory · **thunders,**
and in his temple all · **say,** "Glory!"
The Lord sits enthroned over the · **flood;**
the Lord sits enthroned as king · **for**-ever. R.

Baptism of the Lord – ABC

Psalm 29

Guitar

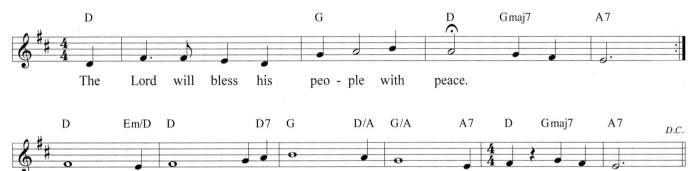

The Lord will bless his peo-ple with peace.

Ascribe to the Lord, O heavenly · **beings,**
ascribe to the Lord glory · **and** strength.
Ascribe to the Lord the glory of his · **name;**
worship the Lord in · **holy** splendour. R.

The voice of the Lord is over the · **waters;**
the Lord, over · **mighty** waters.
The voice of the Lord is · **powerful;**
the voice of the Lord is · **full_of** majesty. R.

The God of glory · **thunders,**
and in his temple all · **say,** "Glory!"
The Lord sits enthroned over the · **flood;**
the Lord sits enthroned as king · **for**-ever. R.

C Instrument

B♭ Instrument

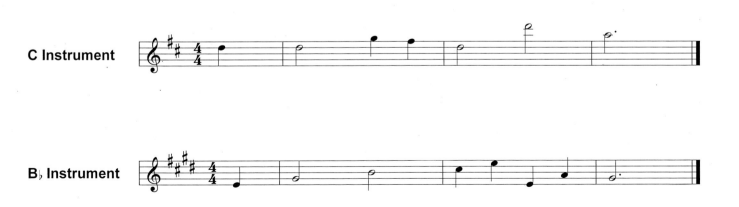

Common Psalm for Lent

Psalm 51

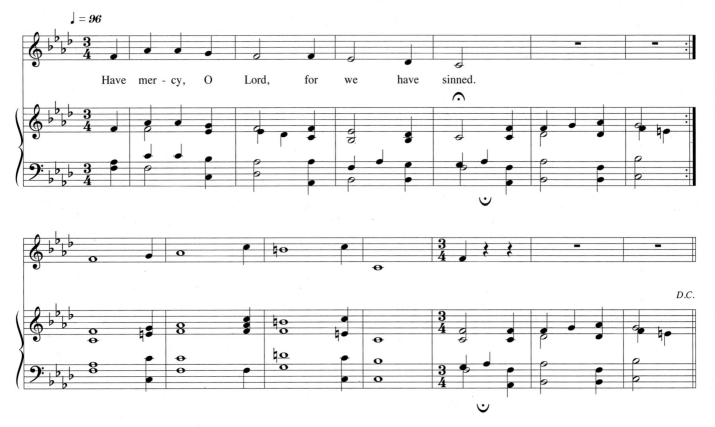

Have mercy, O Lord, for we have sinned.

Have mercy on me, O God, according to your steadfast · **love;**
according to your abundant mercy blot out my trans·-**gressions.**
Wash me thoroughly from my in·-**iquity,**
and cleanse me from my · **sin.** R.

For I know my trans·-**gressions,**
and my sin is ever be·-**fore_me.**
Against you, you alone, have I · **sinned,**
and done what is evil in your · **sight.** R.

Create in me a clean heart, O · **God,**
and put a new and right spirit with·-**in_me.**
Do not cast me away from your · **presence,**
and do not take your holy spirit from · **me.** R.

Restore to me the joy of your sal·-**vation,**
and sustain in me a willing · **spirit.**
O Lord, open my · **lips,**
and my mouth will declare your · **praise.** R.

Common Psalm for Lent

Psalm 51

Guitar

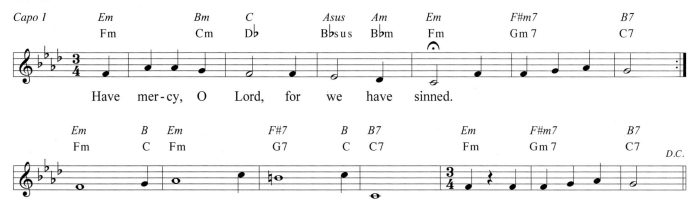

Have mer-cy, O Lord, for we have sinned.

Have mercy on me, O God, according to your steadfast · **love;**
according to your abundant mercy blot out my trans·-**gressions.**
Wash me thoroughly from my in·-**iquity,**
and cleanse me from my · **sin.** R.

For I know my trans·-**gressions,**
and my sin is ever be·-**fore_me.**
Against you, you alone, have I · **sinned,**
and done what is evil in your · **sight.** R.

Create in me a clean heart, O · **God,**
and put a new and right spirit with·-**in_me.**
Do not cast me away from your · **presence,**
and do not take your holy spirit from · **me.** R.

Restore to me the joy of your sal·-**vation,**
and sustain in me a willing · **spirit.**
O Lord, open my · **lips,**
and my mouth will declare your · **praise.** R.

C Instrument

B♭ Instrument

Common Psalm for Lent

Psalm 91

Be with me, Lord, when I am in trou-ble.

You who live in the shelter of the Most · **High,**
who abide in the shadow of the · **Al**-mighty,
will say to the Lord, "My refuge and my · **fortress;**
my God, in whom · **I** trust." R.

No evil shall be·-**fall_you,**
no scourge come near · **your** tent.
For he will command his Angels con·-**cerning_you**
to guard you in all · **your** ways. R.

On their hands they will bear you · **up,**
so that you will not dash your foot against · **a** stone.
You will tread on the lion and the · **adder,**
the young lion and the serpent you will trample · **under** foot. R.

The one who loves me, I will de·-**liver;**
I will protect the one who knows · **my** name.
When he calls to me, I will · **answer_him;**
I will be with him in trouble, I will rescue him · **and** honour_him. R.

Common Psalm for Lent

Psalm 91

Guitar

Be with me, Lord, when I am in trou - ble.

You who live in the shelter of the Most · **High,**
who abide in the shadow of the · **Al**-mighty,
will say to the Lord, "My refuge and my · **fortress;**
my God, in whom · **I** trust." R.

No evil shall be·-**fall_you,**
no scourge come near · **your** tent.
For he will command his Angels con·-**cerning_you**
to guard you in all · **your** ways. R.

On their hands they will bear you · **up,**
so that you will not dash your foot against · **a** stone.
You will tread on the lion and the · **adder,**
the young lion and the serpent you will trample · **under** foot. R.

The one who loves me, I will de·-**liver;**
I will protect the one who knows · **my** name.
When he calls to me, I will · **answer_him;**
I will be with him in trouble, I will rescue him · **and** honour_him. R.

C Instrument

B♭ Instrument

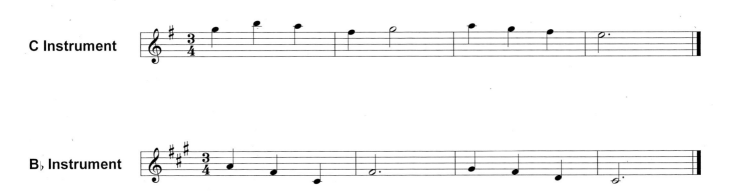

47

Common Psalm for Lent

Psalm 130

With the Lord there is stead-fast love and great pow'r to re-deem.

Out of the depths I cry to you, O · **Lord.**
Lord, hear · **my** voice!
Let your ears be at·-**tentive**
to the voice of my sup·-**pli**-cations! R.

If you, O Lord, should mark in·-**iquities,**
Lord, who · **could** stand?
But there is forgiveness with · **you,**
so that you may be · **re**-vered. R.

I wait for the · **Lord,**
my soul waits, and in his word · **I** hope;
my soul waits for the · **Lord**
more than watchmen for · **the** morning. R.

For with the Lord there is steadfast · **love,**
and with him is great power to · **re**-deem.
It is he who will redeem · **Israel**
from all its · **in**-iquities. R.

Common Psalm for Lent

Psalm 130

Guitar

With the Lord there is stead-fast love   and   great pow'r to re-deem.

Out of the depths I cry to you, O · **Lord.**
Lord, hear · **my** voice!
Let your ears be at·-**tentive**
to the voice of my sup·-**pli**-cations! R.

If you, O Lord, should mark in·-**iquities,**
Lord, who · **could** stand?
But there is forgiveness with · **you,**
so that you may be · **re**-vered. R.

I wait for the · **Lord,**
my soul waits, and in his word · **I** hope;
my soul waits for the · **Lord**
more than watchmen for · **the** morning. R.

For with the Lord there is steadfast · **love,**
and with him is great power to · **re**-deem.
It is he who will redeem · **Israel**
from all its · **in**-iquities. R.

C Instrument

B♭ Instrument

Common Psalm for Holy Week

Psalm 22

All who see me · **mock_at_me;**
they make mouths at me, they shake · **their** heads;
"Commit your cause to the Lord; let him de·-**liver;**
let him rescue the one in whom he · **de**-lights!" R.

For dogs are all a·-**round_me;**
a company of evildoers · **en**-circles_me.
My hands and feet have · **shrivelled;**
I can count all · **my** bones. R.

They divide my clothes a·-**mong_themselves,**
and for my clothing they · **cast** lots.
But you, O Lord, do not be far a·-**way!**
O my help, come quickly · **to_my** aid! R.

I will tell of your name to my brothers and sisters;
   in the midst of the congregation I will · **praise_you:**
You who fear the · **Lord,** praise_him!
All you offspring of Jacob, · **glorify_him;**
stand in awe of him, all you offspring · **of** Israel! R.

50

Common Psalm for Holy Week

Psalm 22

Guitar

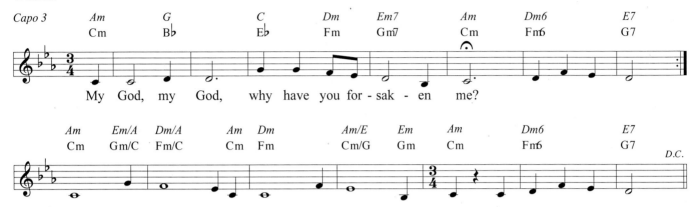

My God, my God, why have you for-sak-en me?

All who see me · **mock_at_me;**
they make mouths at me, they shake · **their** heads;
"Commit your cause to the Lord; let him de·-**liver;**
let him rescue the one in whom he · **de**-lights!" R.

For dogs are all a·-**round_me;**
a company of evildoers · **en**-circles_me.
My hands and feet have · **shrivelled;**
I can count all · **my** bones. R.

They divide my clothes a·-**mong_themselves,**
and for my clothing they · **cast** lots.
But you, O Lord, do not be far a·-**way!**
O my help, come quickly · **to_my** aid! R.

I will tell of your name to my brothers and sisters;
    in the midst of the congregation I will · **praise_you:**
You who fear the · **Lord,** praise_him!
All you offspring of Jacob, · **glorify_him;**
stand in awe of him, all you offspring · **of** Israel! R.

C Instrument

B♭ Instrument

Ash Wednesday – ABC

Psalm 51

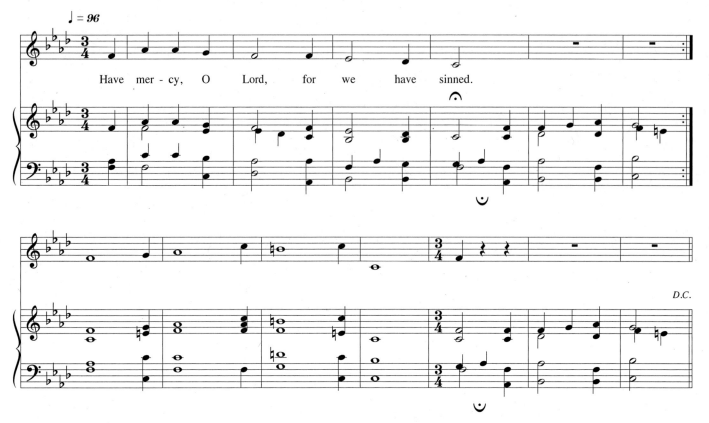

Have mercy, O Lord, for we have sinned.

D.C.

Have mercy on me, O God, according to your steadfast · **love;**
according to your abundant mercy blot out my trans·-**gressions.**
Wash me thoroughly from my in·-**iquity,**
and cleanse me from my · **sin.** R.

For I know my trans·-**gressions,**
and my sin is ever be·-**fore_me.**
Against you, you alone, have I · **sinned,**
and done what is evil in your · **sight.** R.

Create in me a clean heart, O · **God,**
and put a new and right spirit with·-**in_me.**
Do not cast me away from your · **presence,**
and do not take your holy spirit from · **me.** R.

Restore to me the joy of your sal·-**vation,**
and sustain in me a willing · **spirit.**
O Lord, open my · **lips,**
and my mouth will declare your · **praise.** R.

Ash Wednesday – ABC

Psalm 51

Guitar

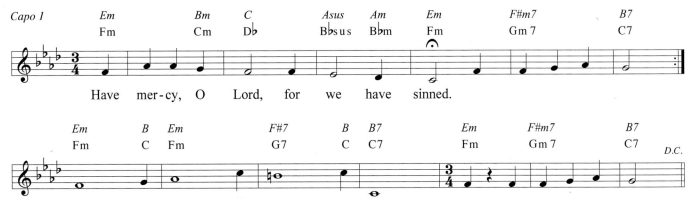

Have mer-cy, O Lord, for we have sinned.

Have mercy on me, O God, according to your steadfast · **love;**
according to your abundant mercy blot out my trans·-**gressions.**
Wash me thoroughly from my in·-**iquity,**
and cleanse me from my · **sin.** R.

For I know my trans·-**gressions,**
and my sin is ever be·-**fore_me.**
Against you, you alone, have I · **sinned,**
and done what is evil in your · **sight.** R.

Create in me a clean heart, O · **God,**
and put a new and right spirit with·-**in_me.**
Do not cast me away from your · **presence,**
and do not take your holy spirit from · **me.** R.

Restore to me the joy of your sal·-**vation,**
and sustain in me a willing · **spirit.**
O Lord, open my · **lips,**
and my mouth will declare your · **praise.** R.

C Instrument

B♭ Instrument

First Sunday of Lent – B

Psalm 25

Your paths, Lord, are love and faith-ful-ness___ for those who keep your cov-e-nant.___

Make me to know your ways, · **O** Lord;
teach · **me** your paths.
Lead me in your · **truth,** and teach_me,
for you are the God of · **my** sal-vation. R.

Be mindful of your mercy, O Lord, and of your stead·-**fast** love,
for they have been · **from** of old.
According to your steadfast · **love** re-member_me,
for the sake of your · **goodness,** O Lord! R.

Good and upright · **is_the** Lord;
therefore he instructs sinners · **in** the way.
He leads the humble in · **what** is right,
and teaches the · **humble** his way. R.

54

First Sunday of Lent – B

Psalm 25

Guitar

Your paths, Lord, are love and faith-ful-ness— for those who keep your cov-e-nant.

Make me to know your ways, · **O** Lord;
teach · **me** your paths.
Lead me in your · **truth,** and teach_me,
for you are the God of · **my** sal-vation. R.

Be mindful of your mercy, O Lord, and of your stead·-**fast** love,
for they have been · **from** of old.
According to your steadfast · **love** re-member_me,
for the sake of your · **goodness,** O Lord! R.

Good and upright · **is_the** Lord;
therefore he instructs sinners · **in** the way.
He leads the humble in · **what** is right,
and teaches the · **humble** his way. R.

C Instrument

B♭ Instrument

Second Sunday of Lent – B

Psalm 116

I will walk be - fore the Lord, in the land of the liv - ing.

I kept my faith, even when I · **said,**
"I am greatly · **af-**flicted."
Precious in the sight of the · **Lord**
is the death of · **his** faithful_ones. R.

O Lord, I am your · **servant.**
You have loosed · **my** bonds.
I will offer to you a thanksgiving · **sacrifice**
and call on the name of · **the** Lord. R.

I will pay my vows to the · **Lord**
in the presence of all · **his** people,
in the courts of the house of the · **Lord,**
in your midst, O · **Je-**rusalem. R.

Second Sunday of Lent – B

Psalm 116

Guitar

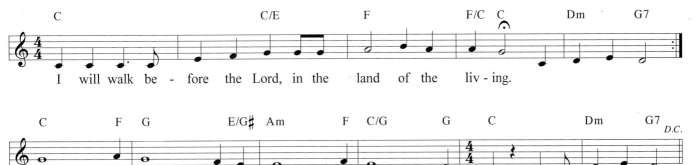

I will walk be - fore the Lord, in the land of the liv - ing.

I kept my faith, even when I · **said,**
"I am greatly · **af**-flicted."
Precious in the sight of the · **Lord**
is the death of · **his** faithful_ones. R.

O Lord, I am your · **servant.**
You have loosed · **my** bonds.
I will offer to you a thanksgiving · **sacrifice**
and call on the name of · **the** Lord. R.

I will pay my vows to the · **Lord**
in the presence of all · **his** people,
in the courts of the house of the · **Lord,**
in your midst, O · **Je**-rusalem. R.

C Instrument

B♭ Instrument

Third Sunday of Lent – B

Psalm 19

Lord, you have the words of e - ter - nal life.

The law of the Lord is · **perfect,**
reviving the · **soul;**
the decrees of the Lord are · **sure,**
making · **wise** the simple. R.

The precepts of the Lord are · **right,**
rejoicing the · **heart;**
the commandment of the Lord is · **clear,**
en·-**lightening** the eyes. R.

The fear of the Lord is · **pure,**
enduring for·-**ever;**
the ordinances of the Lord are · **true**
and righteous · **al**-to-gether. R.

More to be desired are they than · **gold,**
even much fine · **gold;**
sweeter also than · **honey,**
and drippings · **of** the honeycomb. R.

Third Sunday of Lent – B

Psalm 19

Guitar

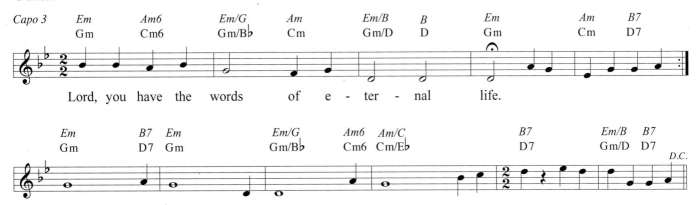

Lord, you have the words of e - ter - nal life.

The law of the Lord is · **perfect,**
reviving the · **soul;**
the decrees of the Lord are · **sure,**
making · **wise** the simple. R.

The precepts of the Lord are · **right,**
rejoicing the · **heart;**
the commandment of the Lord is · **clear,**
en·-**lightening** the eyes. R.

The fear of the Lord is · **pure,**
enduring for·-**ever;**
the ordinances of the Lord are · **true**
and righteous · **al**-to-gether. R.

More to be desired are they than · **gold,**
even much fine · **gold;**
sweeter also than · **honey,**
and drippings · **of** the honeycomb. R.

C Instrument

B♭ Instrument

Third Sunday of Lent (Christian Initiation)

Psalm 95

O come, let us sing to · **the** Lord;
let us make a joyful noise to the rock of our · **sal**-vation!
Let us come into his presence with · **thanks**-giving;
let us make a joyful noise to him with songs · **of** praise! R.

O come, let us worship and · **bow** down,
let us kneel before the Lord, · **our** Maker!
For he is our God, and we are the people of · **his** pasture,
and the sheep of · **his** hand. R.

O that today you would listen to · **his** voice!
Do not harden your hearts, as at Meribah, as on the day at Massah in · **the** wilderness,
when your ancestors tested me, and put me to · **the** proof,
though they had seen · **my** work. R.

Third Sunday of Lent (Christian Initiation)

Psalm 95

Guitar

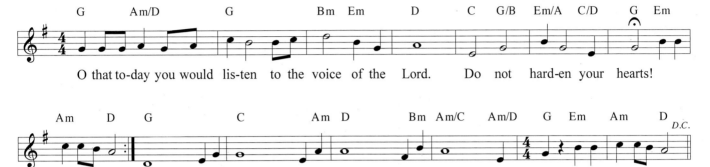

O that to-day you would lis-ten to the voice of the Lord. Do not hard-en your hearts!

O come, let us sing to · **the** Lord;
let us make a joyful noise to the rock of our · **sal**-vation!
Let us come into his presence with · **thanks**-giving;
let us make a joyful noise to him with songs · **of** praise! R.

O come, let us worship and · **bow** down,
let us kneel before the Lord, · **our** Maker!
For he is our God, and we are the people of · **his** pasture,
and the sheep of · **his** hand. R.

O that today you would listen to · **his** voice!
Do not harden your hearts, as at Meribah, as on the day at Massah in · **the** wilderness,
when your ancestors tested me, and put me to · **the** proof,
though they had seen · **my** work. R.

C Instrument

B♭ Instrument

Fourth Sunday of Lent – B

Psalm 137

♩. = 56

Let my tongue cling to my mouth if I do not re - mem - ber you!

D.C.

By the rivers of · **Babylon**—
there we sat down and there · **we** wept
when we remembered · **Zion.**
On the willows there we hung up · **our** harps. R.

For there our · **captors**
asked us · **for** songs,
and our tormentors asked for · **mirth, saying,**
"Sing us one of the songs · **of** Zion!" R.

How could we sing the Lord's · **song**
in a for·-**eign** land?
If I forget you, O Je·-**rusalem,**
let my right · **hand** wither! R.

Let my tongue cling to the roof of my · **mouth,**
if I do not · **re**-member_you,
if I do not set Je·-**rusalem**
above my high·-**est** joy. R.

Fourth Sunday of Lent – B

Psalm 137

Guitar

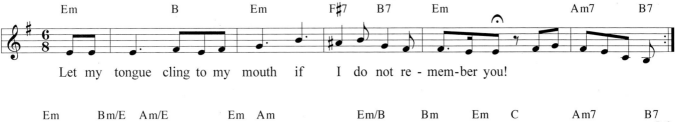

Let my tongue cling to my mouth if I do not re - mem-ber you!

By the rivers of · **Babylon**—
there we sat down and there · **we** wept
when we remembered · **Zion.**
On the willows there we hung up · **our** harps. R.

For there our · **captors**
asked us · **for** songs,
and our tormentors asked for · **mirth,_saying,**
"Sing us one of the songs · **of** Zion!" R.

How could we sing the Lord's · **song**
in a for··**eign** land?
If I forget you, O Je··**rusalem,**
let my right · **hand** wither! R.

Let my tongue cling to the roof of my · **mouth,**
if I do not · **re**-member_you,
if I do not set Je··**rusalem**
above my high··**est** joy. R.

C Instrument

B♭ Instrument

Fourth Sunday of Lent (Christian Initiation)

Psalm 23

The Lord is my shepherd, I shall not want.

The Lord is my shepherd, I shall · **not** want.
He makes me lie down in · **green** pastures;
he leads me be·-**side** still waters;
he re·-**stores** my soul. R.

He leads me in right paths for his · **name's** sake.
Even though I walk through the darkest valley, I fear · **no** evil;
for · **you** are with_me;
your rod and your · **staff**—they comfort_me. R.

You prepare a table · **be**-fore_me
in the presence · **of_my** enemies;
you anoint my · **head** with oil;
my · **cup** over-flows. R.

Surely goodness and mercy · **shall** follow_me
all the days of · **my** life,
and I shall dwell in the · **house_of** the Lord
my · **whole** life long. R.

64

Fourth Sunday of Lent (Christian Initiation)

Psalm 23

Guitar

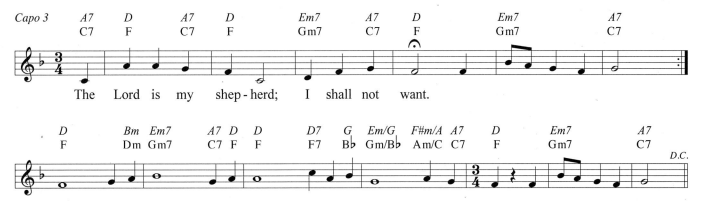

The Lord is my shepherd, I shall · **not** want.
He makes me lie down in · **green** pastures;
he leads me be-·**side** still waters;
he re-·**stores** my soul. R.

He leads me in right paths for his · **name's** sake.
Even though I walk through the darkest valley, I fear · **no** evil;
for · **you** are with_me;
your rod and your · **staff**—they comfort_me. R.

You prepare a table · **be**-fore_me
in the presence · **of_my** enemies;
you anoint my · **head** with oil;
my · **cup** over-flows. R.

Surely goodness and mercy · **shall** follow_me
all the days of · **my** life,
and I shall dwell in the · **house_of** the Lord
my · **whole** life long. R.

C Instrument

B♭ Instrument

Fifth Sunday of Lent – B

Psalm 51

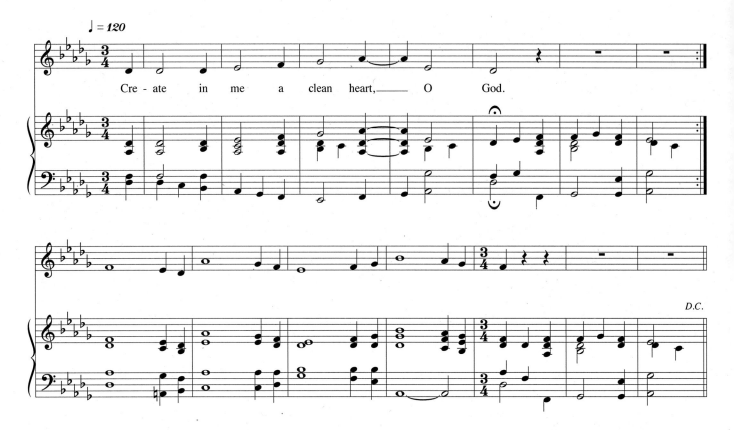

Have mercy on me, O God, according to your stead·-**fast** love;
according to your abundant mercy blot out my · **trans**-gressions.
Wash me thoroughly from my · **in**-iquity,
and cleanse me · **from** my sin. R.

Create in me a clean heart, · **O** God,
and put a new and right spirit · **with**-in_me.
Do not cast me away from · **your** presence,
and do not take your holy · **spirit** from me. R.

Restore to me the joy of your · **sal**-vation,
and sustain in me a will·-**ing** spirit.
Then I will teach transgressors · **your** ways,
and sinners will re·-**turn** to you. R.

Fifth Sunday of Lent – B

Psalm 51

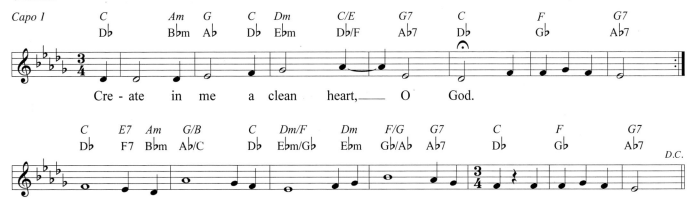

Cre - ate   in   me   a   clean   heart, ____   O   God.

Have mercy on me, O God, according to your stead·-**fast** love;
according to your abundant mercy blot out my · **trans**-gressions.
Wash me thoroughly from my · **in**-iquity,
and cleanse me · **from** my sin. R.

Create in me a clean heart, · **O** God,
and put a new and right spirit · **with**-in_me.
Do not cast me away from · **your** presence,
and do not take your holy · **spirit** from me. R.

Restore to me the joy of your · **sal**-vation,
and sustain in me a will·-**ing** spirit.
Then I will teach transgressors · **your** ways,
and sinners will re·-**turn** to you. R.

Fifth Sunday of Lent (Christian Initiation)

Psalm 130

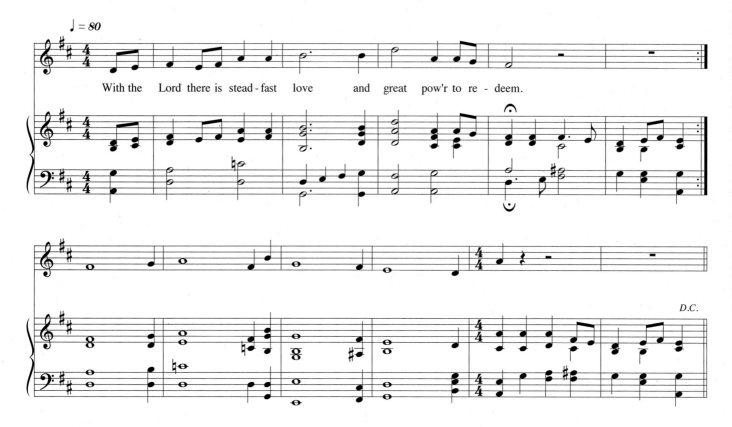

With the Lord there is stead-fast love and great pow'r to re - deem.

Out of the depths I cry to you, O · **Lord.**
Lord, hear · **my** voice!
Let your ears be at·-**tentive**
to the voice of my sup·-**pli**-cations! R.

If you, O Lord, should mark in·-**iquities,**
Lord, who · **could** stand?
But there is forgiveness with · **you,**
so that you may be · **re**-vered. R.

I wait for the · **Lord,**
my soul waits, and in his word · **I** hope;
my soul waits for the · **Lord**
more than watchmen for · **the** morning. R.

For with the Lord there is steadfast · **love,**
and with him is great power to · **re**-deem.
It is he who will redeem · **Israel**
from all its · **in**-iquities. R.

Fifth Sunday of Lent (Christian Initiation)

Psalm 130

Guitar

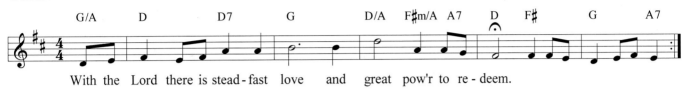

With the Lord there is stead-fast love and great pow'r to re-deem.

Out of the depths I cry to you, O · **Lord.**
Lord, hear · **my** voice!
Let your ears be at·-**tentive**
to the voice of my sup·-**pli**-cations! R.

If you, O Lord, should mark in·-**iquities,**
Lord, who · **could** stand?
But there is forgiveness with · **you,**
so that you may be · **re**-vered. R.

I wait for the · **Lord,**
my soul waits, and in his word · **I** hope;
my soul waits for the · **Lord**
more than watchmen for · **the** morning. R.

For with the Lord there is steadfast · **love,**
and with him is great power to · **re**-deem.
It is he who will redeem · **Israel**
from all its · **in**-iquities. R.

C Instrument

B♭ Instrument

Passion Sunday – B

Psalm 22

My God, my God, why have you for-sak - en me?

All who see me · **mock_at_me;**
they make mouths at me, they shake · **their** heads;
"Commit your cause to the Lord; let him de·-**liver;**
let him rescue the one in whom he · **de-**lights!" R.

For dogs are all a·-**round_me;**
a company of evildoers · **en-**circles_me.
My hands and feet have · **shrivelled;**
I can count all · **my** bones. R.

They divide my clothes a·-**mong_themselves,**
and for my clothing they · **cast** lots.
But you, O Lord, do not be far a·-**way!**
O my help, come quickly · **to_my** aid! R.

I will tell of your name to my brothers and sisters;
    in the midst of the congregation I will · **praise_you:**
You who fear the · **Lord,** praise_him!
All you offspring of Jacob, · **glorify_him;**
stand in awe of him, all you offspring · **of** Israel! R.

Passion Sunday – B
Psalm 22

Guitar

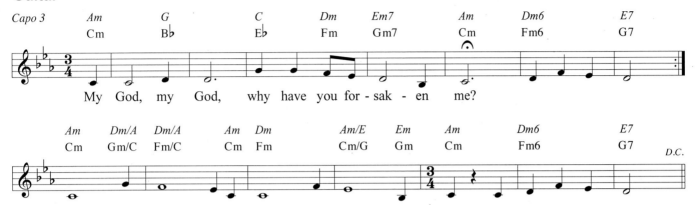

My God, my God, why have you for-sak-en me?

All who see me · **mock_at_me;**
they make mouths at me, they shake · **their** heads;
"Commit your cause to the Lord; let him de·-**liver;**
let him rescue the one in whom he · **de**-lights!" R.

For dogs are all a·-**round_me;**
a company of evildoers · **en**-circles_me.
My hands and feet have · **shrivelled;**
I can count all · **my** bones. R.

They divide my clothes a·-**mong_themselves,**
and for my clothing they · **cast** lots.
But you, O Lord, do not be far a·-**way!**
O my help, come quickly · **to_my** aid! R.

I will tell of your name to my brothers and sisters;
  in the midst of the congregation I will · **praise_you:**
You who fear the · **Lord,** praise_him!
All you offspring of Jacob, · **glorify_him;**
stand in awe of him, all you offspring · **of** Israel! R.

C Instrument

B♭ Instrument

Mass of Chrism – ABC

Psalm 89

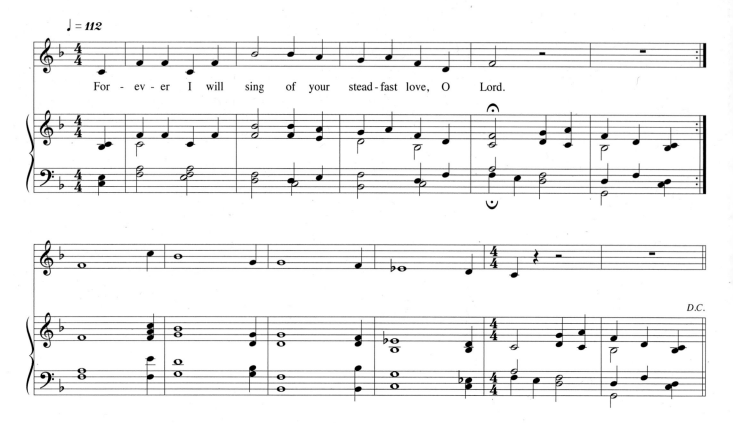

I have found my servant · **David;**
with my holy oil I have a·-**nointed_him;**
my hand shall always re·-**main_with_him;**
my arm also · **shall** strengthen_him. R.

My faithfulness and steadfast love shall be · **with_him;**
and in my name his name shall be ex·-**alted.**
He shall cry to me, "You are my · **Father,**
my God, and the Rock of my · **sal**-vation!" R.

I will make him the · **firstborn,**
the highest of the kings of the · **earth.**
Forever I will keep my steadfast love for · **him,**
and my covenant with him will · **stand** firm. R.

Mass of Chrism – ABC

Psalm 89

Guitar

For - ev - er I will sing of your stead-fast love, O Lord.

I have found my servant · **David;**
with my holy oil I have a·-**nointed_him;**
my hand shall always re·-**main_with_him;**
my arm also · **shall** strengthen_him. R.

My faithfulness and steadfast love shall be · **with_him;**
and in my name his name shall be ex·-**alted.**
He shall cry to me, "You are my · **Father,**
my God, and the Rock of my · **sal**-vation!" R.

I will make him the · **firstborn,**
the highest of the kings of the · **earth.**
Forever I will keep my steadfast love for · **him,**
and my covenant with him will · **stand** firm. R.

C Instrument

B♭ Instrument

Mass of the Lord's Supper – ABC

Psalm 116

The cup of bless-ing that we bless is a shar-ing in the Blood of Christ.

D.C.

What shall I return to the · **Lord**
for all his bounty to · **me?**
I will lift up the cup of sal·-**vation**
and call on the name · **of_the** Lord. R.

Precious in the sight of the · **Lord**
is the death of his · **faithful_ones.**
O Lord, I am your servant, the son of your · **serving_girl.**
You have loosed · **my** bonds. R.

I will offer to you a thanksgiving · **sacrifice**
and call on the name of the · **Lord.**
I will pay my vows to the · **Lord**
in the presence of all · **his** people. R.

Mass of the Lord's Supper – ABC

Psalm 116

Guitar

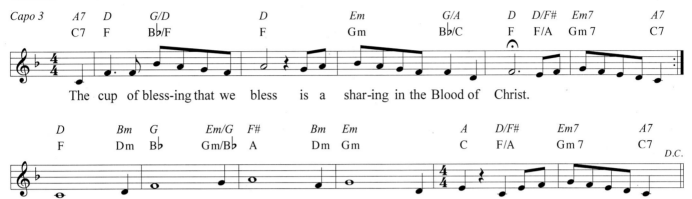

What shall I return to the · **Lord**
for all his bounty to · **me?**
I will lift up the cup of sal·-**vation**
and call on the name · **of_the** Lord. R.

Precious in the sight of the · **Lord**
is the death of his · **faithful_ones.**
O Lord, I am your servant, the son of your · **serving_girl.**
You have loosed · **my** bonds. R.

I will offer to you a thanksgiving · **sacrifice**
and call on the name of the · **Lord.**
I will pay my vows to the · **Lord**
in the presence of all · **his** people. R.

C Instrument

B♭ Instrument

Celebration of the Lord's Passion – ABC

Psalm 31

♩ = 96

Fa-ther, in-to your hands I com-mend my spir - it.

D.C.

In you, O Lord, I seek refuge; do not let me ever be put · **to** shame;
in your righteousness · **de**-liver_me.
Into your hand I commit · **my** spirit;
you have redeemed me, O Lord, · **faith**-ful God. R.

I am the scorn of all my adversaries, a horror to my neighbours, an object of dread to my · **ac**-quaintances.
Those who see me in the · **street** flee_from_me.
I have passed out of mind like one who · **is** dead;
I have become like a · **bro**-ken vessel. R.

But I trust in you, · **O** Lord;
I say, "You are · **my** God."
My times are in · **your** hand;
deliver me from the hand of my · **enemies** and persecutors. R.

Let your face shine upon · **your** servant;
save me in your stead·-**fast** love.
Be strong, and let your heart · **take** courage,
all you who wait · **for** the Lord. R.

Celebration of the Lord's Passion – ABC

Psalm 31

Guitar

Fa-ther, in-to your hands I com-mend my spir - it.

In you, O Lord, I seek refuge; do not let me ever be put · **to** shame;
in your righteousness · **de**-liver_me.
Into your hand I commit · **my** spirit;
you have redeemed me, O Lord, · **faith**-ful God. R.

I am the scorn of all my adversaries, a horror to my neighbours, an object of dread to my · **ac**-quaintances.
Those who see me in the · **street** flee_from_me.
I have passed out of mind like one who · **is** dead;
I have become like a · **bro**-ken vessel. R.

But I trust in you, · **O** Lord;
I say, "You are · **my** God."
My times are in · **your** hand;
deliver me from the hand of my · **enemies** and persecutors. R.

Let your face shine upon · **your** servant;
save me in your stead·-**fast** love.
Be strong, and let your heart · **take** courage,
all you who wait · **for** the Lord. R.

C Instrument

B♭ Instrument

Resurrection of the Lord – Easter Vigil (1.1) – ABC

Psalm 104

Lord, send forth your Spir-it,____ and re - new the face of the earth.

Bless the Lord, O · **my** soul.
O Lord my God, you are very · **great.**
You are clothed with · **honour** and majesty,
wrapped in light as with · **a** garment. R.

You set the earth on its · **foun**-dations,
so that it shall never be · **shaken.**
You cover it with the deep as · **with** a garment;
the waters stood above · **the** mountains. R.

You make springs gush forth in · **the** valleys;
they flow between the · **hills.**
By the streams the birds of the air have their · **ha**-bi-tation;
they sing among · **the** branches. R.

From your lofty abode you water · **the** mountains;
the earth is satisfied with the fruit of your · **work.**
You cause the grass to · **grow_for** the cattle,
and plants for people to use, to bring forth food from · **the** earth. R.

O Lord, how manifold are · **your** works!
In wisdom you have made them · **all;**
the earth is · **full_of** your creatures.
Bless the Lord, O · **my** soul. R.

Resurrection of the Lord – Easter Vigil (1.1) – ABC

Psalm 104

Guitar

Lord, send forth your Spir-it,___ and re - new the face of the earth.

Bless the Lord, O · **my** soul.
O Lord my God, you are very · **great.**
You are clothed with · **honour** and majesty,
wrapped in light as with · **a** garment. R.

You set the earth on its · **foun**-dations,
so that it shall never be · **shaken.**
You cover it with the deep as · **with** a garment;
the waters stood above · **the** mountains. R.

You make springs gush forth in · **the** valleys;
they flow between the · **hills.**
By the streams the birds of the air have their · **ha**-bi-tation;
they sing among · **the** branches. R.

From your lofty abode you water · **the** mountains;
the earth is satisfied with the fruit of your · **work.**
You cause the grass to · **grow_for** the cattle,
and plants for people to use, to bring forth food from · **the** earth. R.

O Lord, how manifold are · **your** works!
In wisdom you have made them · **all;**
the earth is · **full_of** your creatures.
Bless the Lord, O · **my** soul. R.

C Instrument

B♭ Instrument

Resurrection of the Lord – Easter Vigil (1.2) – ABC

Psalm 33

The earth is full of the stead-fast love of the Lord.

The word of the Lord · **is** upright,
and all his work is done · **in** faithfulness.
He loves righteousness · **and** justice;
the earth is full of the steadfast love of · **the** Lord. R.

By the word of the Lord the heavens · **were** made,
and all their host by the breath of · **his** mouth.
He gathered the waters of the sea as in · **a** bottle;
he put the deeps · **in** storehouses. R.

Blessed is the nation whose God is · **the** Lord,
the people whom he has chosen as · **his** heritage.
The Lord looks down · **from** heaven;
he sees all · **human** beings. R.

Our soul waits for · **the** Lord;
he is our help · **and** shield.
Let your steadfast love, O Lord, be · **up**-on_us,
even as we hope · **in** you. R.

Resurrection of the Lord – Easter Vigil (1.2) – ABC

Psalm 33

Guitar

The earth is full of the stead - fast love of the Lord.

The word of the Lord · **is** upright,
and all his work is done · **in** faithfulness.
He loves righteousness · **and** justice;
the earth is full of the steadfast love of · **the** Lord. R.

By the word of the Lord the heavens · **were** made,
and all their host by the breath of · **his** mouth.
He gathered the waters of the sea as in · **a** bottle;
he put the deeps · **in** storehouses. R.

Blessed is the nation whose God is · **the** Lord,
the people whom he has chosen as · **his** heritage.
The Lord looks down · **from** heaven;
he sees all · **human** beings. R.

Our soul waits for · **the** Lord;
he is our help · **and** shield.
Let your steadfast love, O Lord, be · **up**-on_us,
even as we hope · **in** you. R.

C Instrument

B♭ Instrument

Resurrection of the Lord – Easter Vigil (2) – ABC

Psalm 16

Pro - tect me, O God,_____ for in you I take re - fuge._____

The Lord is my chosen portion · **and_my** cup;
you hold · **my** lot.
I keep the Lord always · **be**-fore_me;
because he is at my right hand, I shall · **not** be moved. R.

Therefore my heart is glad, and my soul · **re**-joices;
my body also rests · **se**-cure.
For you do not give me up · **to** Sheol,
or let your faithful one · **see** the Pit. R.

You show me the path · **of** life.
In your presence there is fullness · **of** joy;
in your right hand · **are** pleasures
for·-**ev**-er-more. R.

Resurrection of the Lord – Easter Vigil (2) – ABC

Psalm 16

Guitar

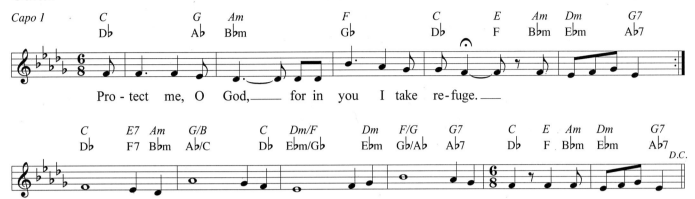

Pro - tect me, O God,＿ for in you I take re-fuge. ＿

The Lord is my chosen portion · **and＿my** cup;
you hold · **my** lot.
I keep the Lord always · **be-fore＿me**;
because he is at my right hand, I shall · **not** be moved. R.

Therefore my heart is glad, and my soul · **re**-joices;
my body also rests · **se**-cure.
For you do not give me up · **to** Sheol,
or let your faithful one · **see** the Pit. R.

You show me the path · **of** life.
In your presence there is fullness · **of** joy;
in your right hand · **are** pleasures
for·-**ev**-er-more. R.

C Instrument

B♭ Instrument

Resurrection of the Lord – Easter Vigil (3) – ABC

Exodus 15

Let us sing—— to the Lord; he has cov-ered him-self in glo-ry.——

I will sing to the Lord, for he has triumphed · **gloriously;**
horse and rider he has thrown into · **the** sea.
The Lord is my strength and my · **might,**
and he has become my · **sal**-vation;
this is my God, and I will · **praise_him,**
my father's God, and I will · **ex**-alt_him. R.

The Lord is a · **warrior;**
the Lord is · **his** name.
Pharaoh's chariots and his army he cast into the · **sea;**
his picked officers were sunk in the · **Red** Sea.
The floods · **covered_them;**
they went down into the depths · **like_a** stone. R.

Your right hand, O Lord, glorious in · **power;** / your right hand, O Lord, shattered · **the** enemy.
In the greatness of your · **majesty** / you overthrew · **your** adversaries;
you sent out your · **fury,** / it consumed them · **like** stubble. R.

You brought your people · **in** / and plant·-**ed** them
on the mountain of your own pos·-**session,** / the place, O Lord, that you made your · **a**-bode,
the sanctuary, O Lord, that your hands have es·-**tablished.** / The Lord will reign forever · **and** ever. R.

Resurrection of the Lord – Easter Vigil (3) – ABC

Exodus 15

Guitar

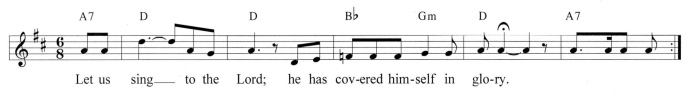

Let us sing___ to the Lord; he has cov-ered him-self in glo-ry.

I will sing to the Lord, for he has triumphed · **gloriously;**
horse and rider he has thrown into · **the** sea.
The Lord is my strength and my · **might,**
and he has become my · **sal**-vation;
this is my God, and I will · **praise_him,**
my father's God, and I will · **ex**-alt_him. R.

The Lord is a · **warrior;** / the Lord is · **his** name.
Pharaoh's chariots and his army he cast into the · **sea;** / his picked officers were sunk in the · **Red** Sea.
The floods · **covered_them;** / they went down into the depths · **like_a** stone. R.

Your right hand, O Lord, glorious in · **power;** / your right hand, O Lord, shattered · **the** enemy.
In the greatness of your · **majesty** / you overthrew · **your** adversaries;
you sent out your · **fury,** / it consumed them · **like** stubble. R.

You brought your people · **in** / and plant-·**ed** them
on the mountain of your own pos·-**session,** / the place, O Lord, that you made your · **a**-bode,
the sanctuary, O Lord, that your hands have es·-**tablished.** / The Lord will reign forever · **and** ever. R.

C Instrument

B♭ Instrument

Resurrection of the Lord – Easter Vigil (4) – ABC

Psalm 30

I will extol you, O Lord, for you have drawn me · **up,**
and did not let my foes rejoice · **over_me.**
O Lord, you brought up my soul from · **Sheol,**
restored me to life from among those gone down · **to_the** Pit. R.

Sing praises to the Lord, O you his · **faithful_ones,**
and give thanks to his holy · **name.**
For his anger is but for a moment; his favour is for a · **lifetime.**
Weeping may linger for the night, but joy comes · **with_the** morning. R.

Hear, O Lord, and be gracious to · **me!**
O Lord, be my · **helper!**
You have turned my mourning into · **dancing.**
O Lord my God, I will give thanks to you · **for**-ever. R.

Resurrection of the Lord – Easter Vigil (4) – ABC

Psalm 30

Guitar

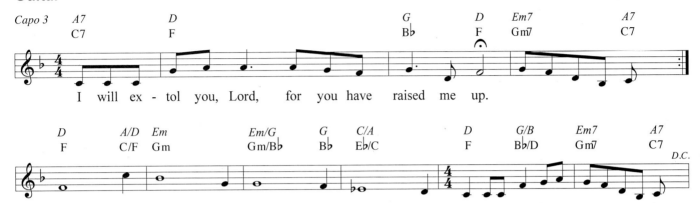

I will ex-tol you, Lord, for you have raised me up.

I will extol you, O Lord, for you have drawn me · **up,**
and did not let my foes rejoice · **over_me.**
O Lord, you brought up my soul from · **Sheol,**
restored me to life from among those gone down · **to_the** Pit. R.

Sing praises to the Lord, O you his · **faithful_ones,**
and give thanks to his holy · **name.**
For his anger is but for a moment; his favour is for a · **lifetime.**
Weeping may linger for the night, but joy comes · **with_the** morning. R.

Hear, O Lord, and be gracious to · **me!**
O Lord, be my · **helper!**
You have turned my mourning into · **dancing.**
O Lord my God, I will give thanks to you · **for**-ever. R.

C Instrument

B♭ Instrument

Resurrection of the Lord – Easter Vigil (5) – ABC

Isaiah 12

With joy you will draw wa-ter___ from the wells of sal - va-tion.

Surely God is my salvation; I will trust, and will not · **be** a-fraid,
for the Lord God is my strength and my might; he has be·-**come_my** sal-vation.
With joy · **you_will** draw water
from the wells · **of** sal-vation. R.

Give thanks · **to** the Lord,
call · **on** his name;
make known his deeds a·-**mong** the nations;
proclaim that his · **name_is** ex-alted. R.

Sing praises to the Lord, for he · **has** done gloriously;
let this be known in · **all** the earth.
Shout aloud and sing for joy, O · **roy**-al Zion,
for great in your midst is the Holy · **One** of Israel. R.

Resurrection of the Lord – Easter Vigil (5) – ABC

Isaiah 12

Guitar

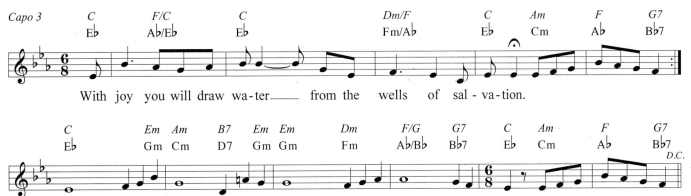

With joy you will draw wa-ter_____ from the wells of sal - va-tion.

Surely God is my salvation; I will trust, and will not · **be** a-fraid,
for the Lord God is my strength and my might; he has be-·**come_my** sal-vation.
With joy · **you_will** draw water
from the wells · **of** sal-vation. R.

Give thanks · **to** the Lord,
call · **on** his name;
make known his deeds a-·**mong** the nations;
proclaim that his · **name_is** ex-alted. R.

Sing praises to the Lord, for he · **has** done gloriously;
let this be known in · **all** the earth.
Shout aloud and sing for joy, O · **roy**-al Zion,
for great in your midst is the Holy · **One** of Israel. R.

C Instrument

B♭ Instrument

Resurrection of the Lord – Easter Vigil (6) – ABC

Psalm 19

Lord, you have the words of e - ter - nal life.

The law of the Lord is · **perfect,**
reviving the · **soul;**
the decrees of the Lord are · **sure,**
making · **wise** the simple. R.

The precepts of the Lord are · **right,**
rejoicing the · **heart;**
the commandment of the Lord is · **clear,**
en·-**lightening** the eyes. R.

The fear of the Lord is · **pure,**
enduring for·-**ever;**
the ordinances of the Lord are · **true**
and righteous · **al**-to-gether. R.

More to be desired are they than · **gold,**
even much fine · **gold;**
sweeter also than · **honey,**
and drippings · **of** the honeycomb. R.

Resurrection of the Lord – Easter Vigil (6) – ABC

Psalm 19

Guitar

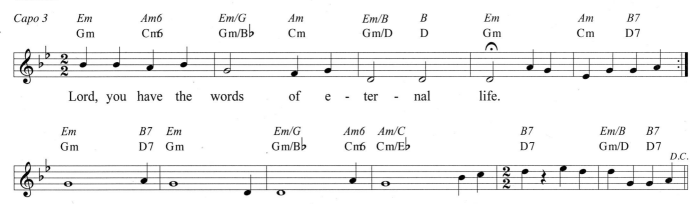

Lord, you have the words of e-ter-nal life.

The law of the Lord is · **perfect,**
reviving the · **soul;**
the decrees of the Lord are · **sure,**
making · **wise** the simple. R.

The precepts of the Lord are · **right,**
rejoicing the · **heart;**
the commandment of the Lord is · **clear,**
en·-**lightening** the eyes. R.

The fear of the Lord is · **pure,**
enduring for·-**ever;**
the ordinances of the Lord are · **true**
and righteous · **al**-to-gether. R.

More to be desired are they than · **gold,**
even much fine · **gold;**
sweeter also than · **honey,**
and drippings · **of** the honeycomb. R.

C Instrument

B♭ Instrument

Resurrection of the Lord – Easter Vigil (7.1) – ABC

Psalm 42

As a deer longs for flow-ing streams, my soul longs for you, O God.

My soul thirsts for · **God,**
for the living · **God.**
When shall I · **come**
and behold the face · **of** God? R.

I went with the · **throng,**
and led them in procession to the house of · **God,**
with glad shouts and songs of · **thanksgiving,**
a multitude · **keeping** festival. R.

O send out your light and your · **truth;**
let them · **lead_me;**
let them bring me to your holy · **mountain**
and to · **your** dwelling. R.

Then I will go to the altar of · **God,**
to God my exceeding · **joy;**
and I will praise you with the · **harp,**
O God, · **my** God. R.

Resurrection of the Lord – Easter Vigil (7.1) – ABC

Psalm 42

Guitar

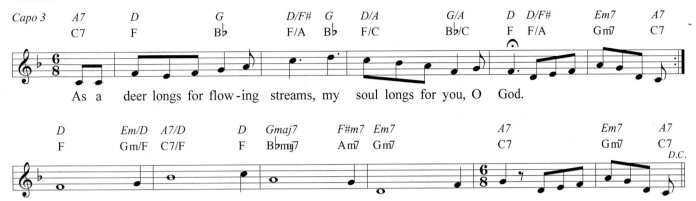

As a deer longs for flow-ing streams, my soul longs for you, O God.

My soul thirsts for · **God,**
for the living · **God.**
When shall I · **come**
and behold the face · **of** God? R.

I went with the · **throng,**
and led them in procession to the house of · **God,**
with glad shouts and songs of · **thanksgiving,**
a multitude · **keeping** festival. R.

O send out your light and your · **truth;**
let them · **lead_me;**
let them bring me to your holy · **mountain**
and to · **your** dwelling. R.

Then I will go to the altar of · **God,**
to God my exceeding · **joy;**
and I will praise you with the · **harp,**
O God, · **my** God. R.

C Instrument

B♭ Instrument

Resurrection of the Lord – Easter Vigil (7.2) – ABC

Psalm 51

Create in me a clean heart, · **O** God,
and put a new and right spirit · **with**-in_me.
Do not cast me away from · **your** presence,
and do not take your holy · **spirit** from me. R.

Restore to me the joy of your · **sal**-vation,
and sustain in me a will·-**ing** spirit.
Then I will teach transgressors · **your** ways,
and sinners will re·-**turn** to you. R.

For you have no delight · **in** sacrifice;
if I were to give a burnt offering, you would not · **be** pleased.
The sacrifice acceptable to God is a bro·-**ken** spirit;
a broken and contrite heart, O God, you will · **not** de-spise. R.

Resurrection of the Lord – Easter Vigil (7.2) – ABC

Psalm 51

Guitar

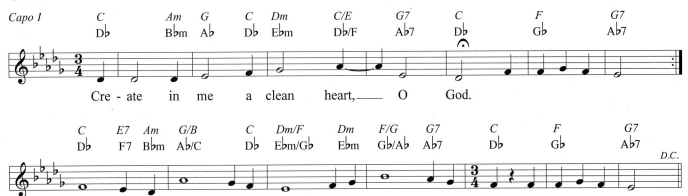

Create in me a clean heart,· **O** God,
and put a new and right spirit · **with**-in_me.
Do not cast me away from · **your** presence,
and do not take your holy · **spirit** from me. R.

Restore to me the joy of your · **sal**-vation,
and sustain in me a will·-**ing** spirit.
Then I will teach transgressors · **your** ways,
and sinners will re·-**turn** to you. R.

For you have no delight · **in** sacrifice;
if I were to give a burnt offering, you would not · **be** pleased.
The sacrifice acceptable to God is a bro·-**ken** spirit;
a broken and contrite heart, O God, you will · **not** de-spise. R.

C Instrument

Bb Instrument

Resurrection of the Lord – Easter Vigil – Solemn Alleluia – ABC

Psalm 118

O give thanks to the Lord, for · **he** is good;
his steadfast love en·-**dures** for-ever.
Let Is·-**rael** say,
"His steadfast love en·-**dures** for-ever." R.

"The right hand of the Lord · **is** ex-alted;
the right hand of the · **Lord** does valiantly."
I shall not die, but · **I_shall** live,
and recount the · **deeds_of** the Lord. R.

The stone that the · **builders** re-jected
has become · **the** chief cornerstone.
This is the · **Lord's** doing;
it is marvellous · **in** our eyes. R.

Resurrection of the Lord – Easter Vigil – Solemn Alleluia – ABC

Psalm 118

Guitar

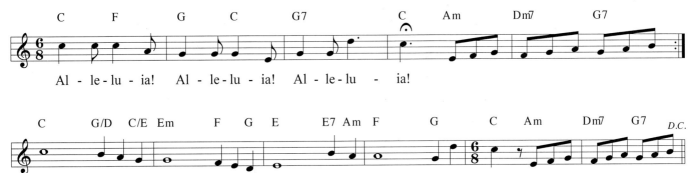

O give thanks to the Lord, for · **he** is good;
his steadfast love en·-**dures** for-ever.
Let Is·-**rael** say,
"His steadfast love en·-**dures** for-ever." R.

"The right hand of the Lord · **is** ex-alted;
the right hand of the · **Lord** does valiantly."
I shall not die, but · **I_shall** live,
and recount the · **deeds_of** the Lord. R.

The stone that the · **builders** re-jected
has become · **the** chief cornerstone.
This is the · **Lord's** doing;
it is marvellous · **in** our eyes. R.

Resurrection of the Lord – Easter Sunday – ABC

Psalm 118

This is the day the Lord has made; let us re-joice and be glad.

O give thanks to the Lord, for · **he** is good;
his steadfast love en·-**dures** for-ever.
Let Is·-**rael** say,
"His steadfast love en·-**dures** for-ever." R.

"The right hand of the Lord · **is** ex-alted;
the right hand of the · **Lord** does valiantly."
I shall not die, but · **I_shall** live,
and recount the · **deeds_of** the Lord. R.

The stone that the · **builders** re-jected
has become · **the** chief cornerstone.
This is the · **Lord's** doing;
it is marvellous · **in** our eyes. R.

Resurrection of the Lord – Easter Sunday – ABC

Psalm 118

Guitar

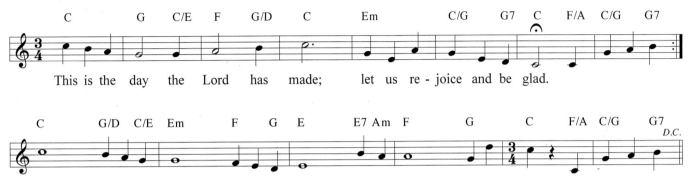

This is the day the Lord has made; let us re - joice and be glad.

O give thanks to the Lord, for · **he** is good;
his steadfast love en·-**dures** for-ever.
Let Is·-**rael** say,
"His steadfast love en·-**dures** for-ever." R.

"The right hand of the Lord · **is** ex-alted;
the right hand of the · **Lord** does valiantly."
I shall not die, but · **I_shall** live,
and recount the · **deeds_of** the Lord. R.

The stone that the · **builders** re-jected
has become · **the** chief cornerstone.
This is the · **Lord's** doing;
it is marvellous · **in** our eyes. R.

C Instrument

B♭ Instrument

Common Psalm for Easter

Psalm 118

O give thanks to the Lord, for · **he** is good;
his steadfast love en·-**dures** for-ever.
Let Is·-**rael** say,
"His steadfast love en·-**dures** for-ever." R.

"The right hand of the Lord · **is** ex-alted;
the right hand of the · **Lord** does valiantly."
I shall not die, but · **I_shall** live,
and recount the · **deeds_of** the Lord. R.

The stone that the · **builders** re-jected
has become · **the** chief cornerstone.
This is the · **Lord's** doing;
it is marvellous · **in** our eyes. R.

Common Psalm for Easter

Psalm 118

Guitar

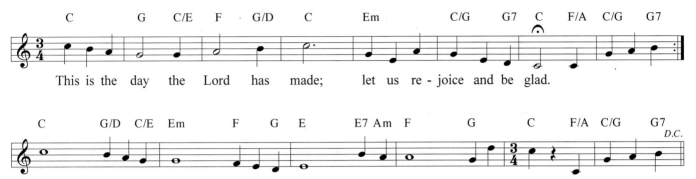

This is the day the Lord has made; let us re - joice and be glad.

O give thanks to the Lord, for · **he** is good;
his steadfast love en·-**dures** for-ever.
Let Is·-**rael** say,
"His steadfast love en·-**dures** for-ever." R.

"The right hand of the Lord · **is** ex-alted;
the right hand of the · **Lord** does valiantly."
I shall not die, but · **I_shall** live,
and recount the · **deeds_of** the Lord. R.

The stone that the · **builders** re-jected
has become · **the** chief cornerstone.
This is the · **Lord's** doing;
it is marvellous · **in** our eyes. R.

C Instrument

B♭ Instrument

Common Psalm for Easter

Psalm 66

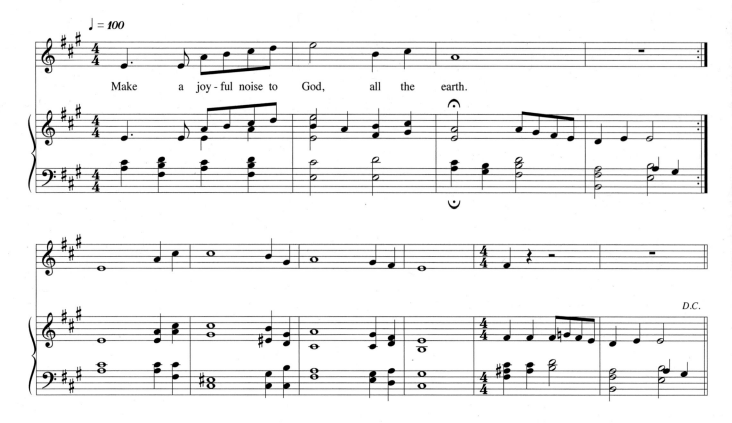

Make a joyful noise to God, all · **the** earth;
sing the glory · **of_his** name;
give to him · **glorious** praise.
Say to God, "How awesome are your · **deeds!**" R.

"All the earth · **worships** you;
they sing praises to you, sing praises · **to_your** name."
Come and see what God · **has** done:
he is awesome in his deeds among the children of · **Adam.** R.

He turned the sea into · **dry** land;
they passed through the river · **on** foot.
There we rejoiced · **in** him,
who rules by his might for-·**ever.** R.

Come and hear, all you who · **fear** God,
and I will tell what he · **has** done_for_me.
Blessed be God, because he has not rejected · **my** prayer
or removed his steadfast love from · **me.** R.

Common Psalm for Easter

Psalm 66

Guitar

Make a joy-ful noise to God, all the earth.

Make a joyful noise to God, all · **the** earth;
sing the glory · **of_his** name;
give to him · **glorious** praise.
Say to God, "How awesome are your · **deeds!**" R.

"All the earth · **worships** you;
they sing praises to you, sing praises · **to_your** name."
Come and see what God · **has** done:
he is awesome in his deeds among the children of · **Adam.** R.

He turned the sea into · **dry** land;
they passed through the river · **on** foot.
There we rejoiced · **in** him,
who rules by his might for·-**ever.** R.

Come and hear, all you who · **fear** God,
and I will tell what he · **has** done_for_me.
Blessed be God, because he has not rejected · **my** prayer
or removed his steadfast love from · **me.** R.

C Instrument

B♭ Instrument

Common Psalm for after Ascension

Psalm 47

God has gone up with a shout,_____ the Lord with the sound of a trum-pet._____

Clap your hands, all · **you** peoples;
shout to God with loud songs · **of** joy.
For the Lord, the Most High, · **is** awesome,
a great king over · **all** the earth. R.

God has gone up · **with_a** shout,
the Lord with the sound of · **a** trumpet.
Sing praises to God, · **sing** praises;
sing praises to our · **King,** sing praises. R.

For God is the king of all · **the** earth;
sing praises · **with_a** Psalm.
God is king over · **the** nations;
God sits on his · **ho**-ly throne. R.

Common Psalm for after Ascension

Psalm 47

Guitar

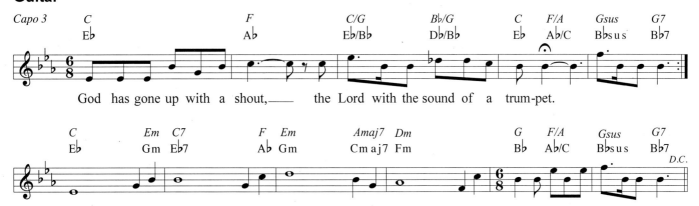

God has gone up with a shout,—— the Lord with the sound of a trum-pet.

Clap your hands, all · **you** peoples;
shout to God with loud songs · **of** joy.
For the Lord, the Most High, · **is** awesome,
a great king over · **all** the earth. R.

God has gone up · **with_a** shout,
the Lord with the sound of · **a** trumpet.
Sing praises to God, · **sing** praises;
sing praises to our · **King,** sing praises. R.

For God is the king of all · **the** earth;
· sing praises · **with_a** Psalm.
God is king over · **the** nations;
God sits on his · **ho**-ly throne. R.

C Instrument

B♭ Instrument

Common Psalm for Pentecost

Psalm 104

Lord, send forth your Spir-it,——— and re - new the face of the earth.

Bless the Lord, O · **my** soul.
O Lord my God, you are very · **great.**
O Lord, how manifold · **are** your works!
The earth is full of · **your** creatures. R.

When you take away · **their** breath,
they die and return to their · **dust.**
When you send forth your spirit, they · **are** cre-ated;
and you renew the face of · **the** earth. R.

May the glory of the Lord endure · **for-**ever;
may the Lord rejoice in his · **works—**
May my meditation be · **pleasing** to him,
for I rejoice in · **the** Lord. R.

Common Psalm for Pentecost
Psalm 104

Bless the Lord, O · **my** soul.
O Lord my God, you are very · **great.**
O Lord, how manifold · **are** your works!
The earth is full of · **your** creatures. R.

When you take away · **their** breath,
they die and return to their · **dust.**
When you send forth your spirit, they · **are** cre-ated;
and you renew the face of · **the** earth. R.

May the glory of the Lord endure · **for-**ever;
may the Lord rejoice in his · **works—**
May my meditation be · **pleasing** to him,
for I rejoice in · **the** Lord. R.

Second Sunday of Easter – B

Psalm 118

Give thanks to the Lord, for he is good; his stead-fast love en-dures for-ev-er.

Let Israel · **say,**
"His steadfast love endures for·-**ever**."
Let the house of Aaron · **say,**
"His steadfast love endures for·-**ever**."
Let those who fear the Lord · **say,**
"His steadfast love endures for·-**ever**." R.

"The right hand of the Lord is ex·-**alted;**
the right hand of the Lord does · **valiantly**."
I shall not die, but I shall · **live,**
and recount the deeds of the · **Lord.**
The Lord has punished me se·-**verely,**
but he did not give me over to · **death.** R.

The stone that the builders re·-**jected**
has become the chief · **cornerston**e.
This is the Lord's · **doing;**
it is marvellous in our · **eyes.**
This is the day that the Lord has · **made;**
let us rejoice and be glad in · **it.** R.

Second Sunday of Easter – B

Psalm 118

Guitar

Give thanks to the Lord, for he is good; his stead-fast love en-dures for-ev-er.

Let Israel · **say,**
"His steadfast love endures for-·**ever.**"
Let the house of Aaron · **say,**
"His steadfast love endures for-·**ever.**"
Let those who fear the Lord · **say,**
"His steadfast love endures for-·**ever.**" R.

"The right hand of the Lord is ex-·**alted;**
the right hand of the Lord does · **valiantly.**"
I shall not die, but I shall · **live,**
and recount the deeds of the · **Lord.**
The Lord has punished me se-·**verely,**
but he did not give me over to · **death.** R.

The stone that the builders re-·**jected**
has become the chief · **cornerstone.**
This is the Lord's · **doing;**
it is marvellous in our · **eyes.**
This is the day that the Lord has · **made;**
let us rejoice and be glad in · **it.** R.

C Instrument

B♭ Instrument

Third Sunday of Easter – B

Psalm 4

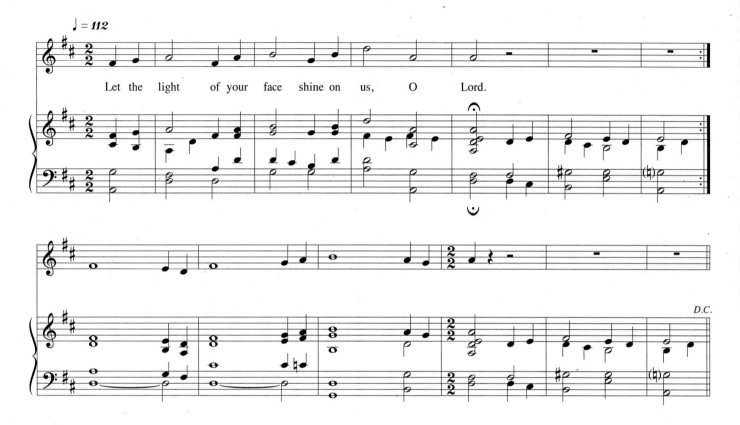

♩ = 112

Let the light of your face shine on us, O Lord.

D.C.

Answer me when I call, O God of · **my** right!
You gave me room when I was in · **dis**-tress.
Be gracious to me, and · **hear** my prayer. R.

But know that the Lord has set · **a**-part
the faithful for · **him**-self;
the Lord hears when I · **call** to him. R.

There are many · **who** say,
"O that we might see · **some** good!
Let the light of your face shine on · **us,** O Lord!" R.

I will both lie down and sleep · **in** peace;
for you alone, · **O** Lord,
make me lie · **down** in safety. R.

Third Sunday of Easter – B

Psalm 4

Guitar

Let the light of your face shine on us, O Lord.

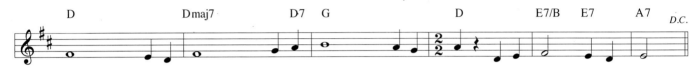

Answer me when I call, O God of · **my** right!
You gave me room when I was in · **dis**-tress.
Be gracious to me, and · **hear** my prayer. R.

But know that the Lord has set · **a**-part
the faithful for · **him**-self;
the Lord hears when I · **call** to him. R.

There are many · **who** say,
"O that we might see · **some** good!
Let the light of your face shine on · **us,** O Lord!" R.

I will both lie down and sleep · **in** peace;
for you alone, · **O** Lord,
make me lie · **down** in safety. R.

C Instrument

Bb Instrument

Fourth Sunday of Easter – B

Psalm 118

O give thanks to the Lord, for he is · **good;**
his steadfast love endures · **for**-ever!
It is better to take refuge in the · **Lord**
than to put confidence · **in** humans.
It is better to take refuge in the · **Lord**
than to put confidence · **in** princes. R.

I thank you that you have · **answered_me**
and have become my · **sal**-vation.
The stone that the builders re·-**jected**
has become the · **chief** cornerstone.
This is the Lord's · **doing;**
it is marvellous in · **our** eyes. R.

Blessed is the one who comes in the name of the · **Lord.**
We bless you from the house of · **the** Lord.
You are my God, and I will give · **thanks_to_you;**
you are my God, I will · **ex**-tol_you.
O give thanks to the Lord, for he is · **good,**
for his steadfast love endures · **for**-ever. R.

Fourth Sunday of Easter – B

Psalm 118

Guitar

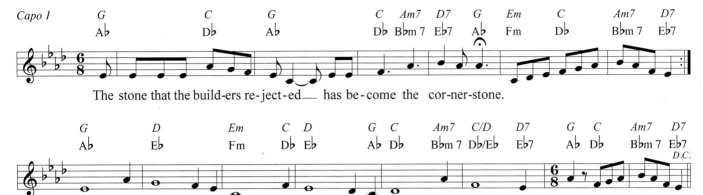

O give thanks to the Lord, for he is · **good;**
his steadfast love endures · **for**-ever!
It is better to take refuge in the · **Lord**
than to put confidence · **in** humans.
It is better to take refuge in the · **Lord**
than to put confidence · **in** princes. R.

I thank you that you have · **answered_me**
and have become my · **sal**-vation.
The stone that the builders re·-**jected**
has become the · **chief** cornerstone.
This is the Lord's · **doing;**
it is marvellous in · **our** eyes. R.

Blessed is the one who comes in the name of the · **Lord.**
We bless you from the house of · **the** Lord.
You are my God, and I will give · **thanks_to_you;**
you are my God, I will · **ex**-tol_you.
O give thanks to the Lord, for he is · **good,**
for his steadfast love endures · **for**-ever. R.

C Instrument

B♭ Instrument

Fifth Sunday of Easter – B

Psalm 22

Lord, from you comes my praise in the great con-gre-ga-tion.

My vows I will pay before those who · **fear_him.**
The poor shall eat · **and** be satisfied;
those who seek him shall · **praise** the Lord.
May your hearts live · **for**-ever. R.

All the ends of the earth shall remember and turn to the · **Lord;**
and all the families of the nations shall wor·-**ship** be-fore_him.
To him, indeed, shall all who sleep in the · **earth** bow down;
before him shall bow all who go down to · **the** dust. R.

I shall live for him. Posterity will · **serve_him;**
future generations will be told a·-**bout** the Lord,
and proclaim his deliverance to a people · **yet** un-born,
saying that he · **has** done_it. R.

Fifth Sunday of Easter – B April 29, 2018

Psalm 22

Guitar

Lord, from you comes my praise in the great con - gre - ga - tion.

My vows I will pay before those who · **fear_him.**
The poor shall eat · **and** be satisfied;
those who seek him shall · **praise** the Lord.
May your hearts live · **for**-ever. R.

All the ends of the earth shall remember and turn to the · **Lord;**
and all the families of the nations shall wor·-**ship** be-fore_him.
To him, indeed, shall all who sleep in the · **earth** bow down;
before him shall bow all who go down to · **the** dust. R.

I shall live for him. Posterity will · **serve_him;**
future generations will be told a·-**bout** the Lord,
and proclaim his deliverance to a people · **yet** un-born,
saying that he · **has** done_it. R.

C Instrument

B♭ Instrument

Sixth Sunday of Easter – B

Psalm 98

O sing to the Lord · **a** new song,
for he has done · **marvel**-lous things.
His right hand and his · **ho**-ly arm
have · **brought** him victory. R.

The Lord has made · **known** his victory;
he has revealed his vindication in the · **sight_of** the nations.
He has remembered his · **stead**-fast love
and faithfulness to the · **house** of Israel. R.

All the ends of the · **earth** have seen
the victory · **of** our God.
Make a joyful noise to the Lord, · **all** the earth;
break forth into joyous · **song_and** sing praises. R.

Sixth Sunday of Easter – B

Psalm 98

Guitar

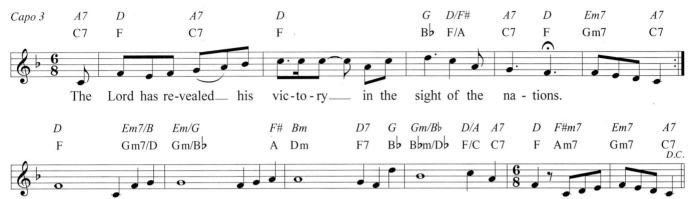

The Lord has re-vealed— his vic-to-ry—— in the sight of the na - tions.

O sing to the Lord · **a** new song,
for he has done · **marvel**-lous things.
His right hand and his · **ho**-ly arm
have · **brought** him victory. R.

The Lord has made · **known** his victory;
he has revealed his vindication in the · **sight_of** the nations.
He has remembered his · **stead**-fast love
and faithfulness to the · **house** of Israel. R.

All the ends of the · **earth** have seen
the victory · **of** our God.
Make a joyful noise to the Lord, · **all** the earth;
break forth into joyous · **song_and** sing praises. R.

C Instrument

B♭ Instrument

Ascension of the Lord – B

Psalm 47

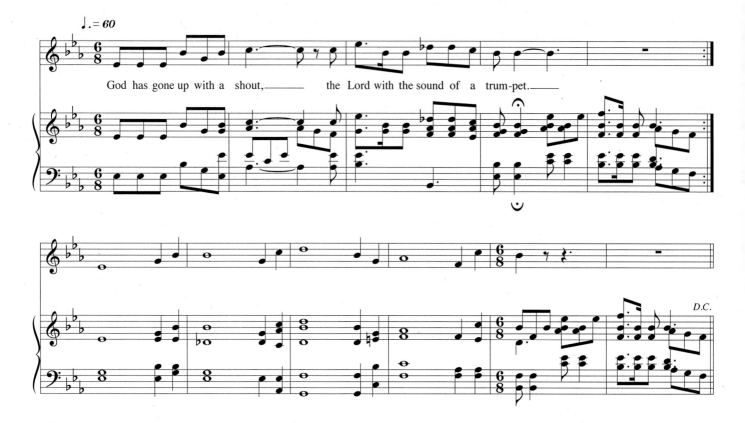

God has gone up with a shout,_____ the Lord with the sound of a trum-pet._____

Clap your hands, all · **you** peoples;
shout to God with loud songs · **of** joy.
For the Lord, the Most High, · **is** awesome,
a great king over · **all** the earth. R.

God has gone up · **with_a** shout,
the Lord with the sound of · **a** trumpet.
Sing praises to God, · **sing** praises;
sing praises to our · **King,** sing praises. R.

For God is the king of all · **the** earth;
sing praises · **with_a** Psalm.
God is king over · **the** nations;
God sits on his · **ho**-ly throne. R.

Ascension of the Lord – B
Psalm 47

May 13, 2018

Guitar

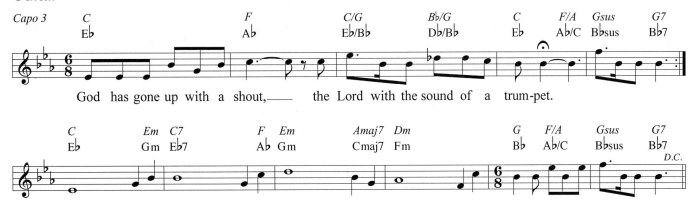

God has gone up with a shout,— the Lord with the sound of a trum-pet.

Clap your hands, all · **you** peoples;
shout to God with loud songs · **of** joy.
For the Lord, the Most High, · **is** awesome,
a great king over · **all** the earth. R.

God has gone up · **with_a** shout,
the Lord with the sound of · **a** trumpet.
Sing praises to God, · **sing** praises;
sing praises to our · **King,** sing praises. R.

For God is the king of all · **the** earth;
sing praises · **with_a** Psalm.
God is king over · **the** nations;
God sits on his · **ho**-ly throne. R.

C Instrument

B♭ Instrument

Seventh Sunday of Easter – B

Psalm 103

The Lord has es-tab-lished his throne in the heav-ens.

Bless the Lord, O my · **soul,**
and all that is within me, bless his · **holy** name.
Bless the Lord, O my · **soul,**
and do not forget all · **his** benefits. R.

For as the heavens are high above the · **earth,**
so great is his steadfast love toward those · **who** fear_him;
as far as the east is from the · **west,**
so far he removes our transgressions · **from** us. R.

The Lord has established his throne in the · **heavens,**
and his kingdom rules · **over** all.
Bless the Lord, O you his · **Angels,**
you mighty ones who do his bidding, obedient to his · **spoken** word. R.

Seventh Sunday of Easter – B

Psalm 103

Guitar

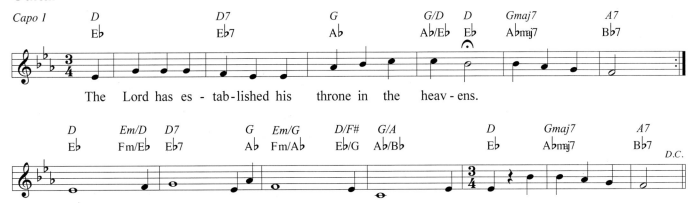

The Lord has es - tab-lished his throne in the heav - ens.

Bless the Lord, O my · **soul,**
and all that is within me, bless his · **holy** name.
Bless the Lord, O my · **soul,**
and do not forget all · **his** benefits. R.

For as the heavens are high above the · **earth,**
so great is his steadfast love toward those · **who** fear_him;
as far as the east is from the · **west,**
so far he removes our transgressions · **from** us. R.

The Lord has established his throne in the · **heavens,**
and his kingdom rules · **over** all.
Bless the Lord, O you his · **Angels,**
you mighty ones who do his bidding, obedient to his · **spoken** word. R.

C Instrument

B♭ Instrument

Pentecost (Vigil) – ABC

Psalm 104

Lord, send forth your Spir-it,—— and re-new the face of the earth.

Bless the Lord, O · **my** soul.
O Lord my God, you are very · **great.**
You are clothed with · **honour** and majesty,
wrapped in light as with · **a** garment. R.

O Lord, how manifold are · **your** works!
In wisdom you have made them · **all;**
the earth is · **full_of** your creatures,
living things both small · **and** great. R.

These all look · **to** you
to give them their food in due · **season;**
when you give to them, they · **gather** it up;
when you open your hand, they are filled with · **good** things. R.

When you take away · **their** breath,
they die and return to their · **dust.**
When you send forth your spirit, they · **are** cre-ated;
and you renew the face of · **the** earth. R.

For Pentecost Sunday, turn to page 138.

Pentecost (Vigil) – ABC

Psalm 104

Guitar

Lord, send forth your Spir-it,___ and re - new the face of the earth.

Bless the Lord, O · **my** soul.
O Lord my God, you are very · **great.**
You are clothed with · **honour** and majesty,
wrapped in light as with · **a** garment. R.

O Lord, how manifold are · **your** works!
In wisdom you have made them · **all;**
the earth is · **full_of** your creatures,
living things both small · **and** great. R.

These all look · **to** you
to give them their food in due · **season;**
when you give to them, they · **gather** it up;
when you open your hand, they are filled with · **good** things. R.

When you take away · **their** breath,
they die and return to their · **dust.**
When you send forth your spirit, they · **are** cre-ated;
and you renew the face of · **the** earth. R.

C Instrument

B♭ Instrument

123

Extended Vigil of Pentecost (1) – ABC

Psalm 8

O Lord, our God, you have giv-en us the breath of life!

When I look at your heavens, the work of · **your** fingers,
the moon and the stars that you have · **es**-tablished;
what is a man that you · **are** mindful_of_him,
or the son of man · **that** you care_for_him? R.

Yet you have made him a little lower · **than_the** Angels,
and crowned him with glory · **and** honour.
You have given him dominion over the works of · **your** hands;
you have put all things · **under** his feet. R.

All sheep · **and** oxen,
and also the beasts of · **the** field,
the birds of the air, and the fish of · **the** sea,
whatever passes along the · **paths_of** the seas. R.

Extended Vigil of Pentecost (1) – ABC

Psalm 8

Guitar

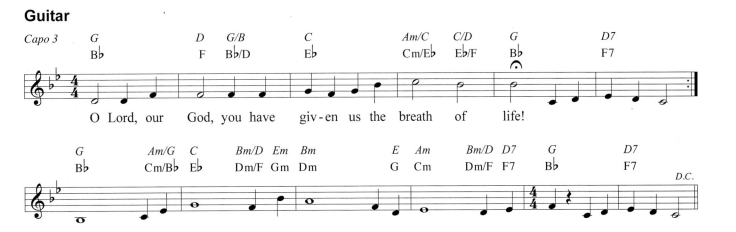

O Lord, our God, you have giv-en us the breath of life!

When I look at your heavens, the work of · **your** fingers,
the moon and the stars that you have · **es**-tablished;
what is a man that you · **are** mindful_of_him,
or the son of man · **that** you care_for_him? R.

Yet you have made him a little lower · **than_the** Angels,
and crowned him with glory · **and** honour.
You have given him dominion over the works of · **your** hands;
you have put all things · **under** his feet. R.

All sheep · **and** oxen,
and also the beasts of · **the** field,
the birds of the air, and the fish of · **the** sea,
whatever passes along the · **paths_of** the seas. R.

C Instrument

B♭ Instrument

Extended Vigil of Pentecost (2) – ABC

Psalm 80

Give ear, O Shepherd · **of** Israel,
you who are enthroned upon the cherubim, shine · **forth.**
Stir up your · **might,**
and come to · **save_us.** R.

Restore us, · **O** God;
let your face shine, that we may be · **saved.**
O Lord God of · **hosts,**
how long will you be angry with your people's · **prayers?** R.

Turn again, O God · **of** hosts;
look down from heaven, and · **see.**
Then we will never turn · **back_from_you;**
give us life, and we will call on your · **name.** R.

Extended Vigil of Pentecost (2) – ABC

Psalm 80

Guitar

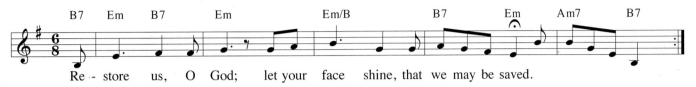

Re - store us, O God; let your face shine, that we may be saved.

Give ear, O Shepherd · **of** Israel,
you who are enthroned upon the cherubim, shine · **forth.**
Stir up your · **might,**
and come to · **save_us.** R.

Restore us, · **O** God;
let your face shine, that we may be · **saved.**
O Lord God of · **hosts,**
how long will you be angry with your people's · **prayers?** R.

Turn again, O God · **of** hosts;
look down from heaven, and · **see.**
Then we will never turn · **back_from_you;**
give us life, and we will call on your · **name.** R.

C Instrument

B♭ Instrument

Extended Vigil of Pentecost (3) – ABC

Psalm 97

The Lord is king! Let the earth re·-**joice;**
let the many coastlands · **be** glad!
Clouds and thick darkness are · **all** a-round_him;
righteousness and justice are the foundation · **of** his throne. R.

Fire goes be·-**fore_him,**
and consumes his adversaries on · **every** side.
His lightnings light · **up** the world;
the earth · **sees** and trembles. R.

The mountains melt like wax before the · **Lord,**
before the Lord of · **all_the** earth.
The heavens pro·-**claim** his righteousness;
and all the peoples be·-**hold** his glory. R.

Light dawns for the · **righteous,**
and joy for the upright · **in** heart.
Rejoice in the Lord, · **O** you righteous,
and give thanks to his · **ho**-ly name! R.

Extended Vigil of Pentecost (3) – ABC

Psalm 97

Guitar

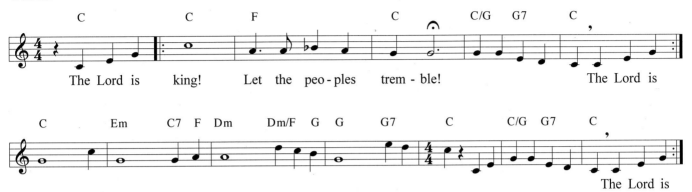

The Lord is king! Let the peo-ples trem-ble! The Lord is

The Lord is

The Lord is king! Let the earth re-·**joice;**
let the many coastlands · **be** glad!
Clouds and thick darkness are · **all** a-round_him;
righteousness and justice are the foundation · **of** his throne. R.

Fire goes be-·**fore_him,**
and consumes his adversaries on · **every** side.
His lightnings light · **up** the world;
the earth · **sees** and trembles. R.

The mountains melt like wax before the · **Lord,**
before the Lord of · **all_the** earth.
The heavens pro-·**claim** his righteousness;
and all the peoples be-·**hold** his glory. R.

Light dawns for the · **righteous,**
and joy for the upright · **in** heart.
Rejoice in the Lord, · **O** you righteous,
and give thanks to his · **ho**-ly name! R.

C Instrument

B♭ Instrument

Extended Vigil of Pentecost (4) – ABC

Psalm 139

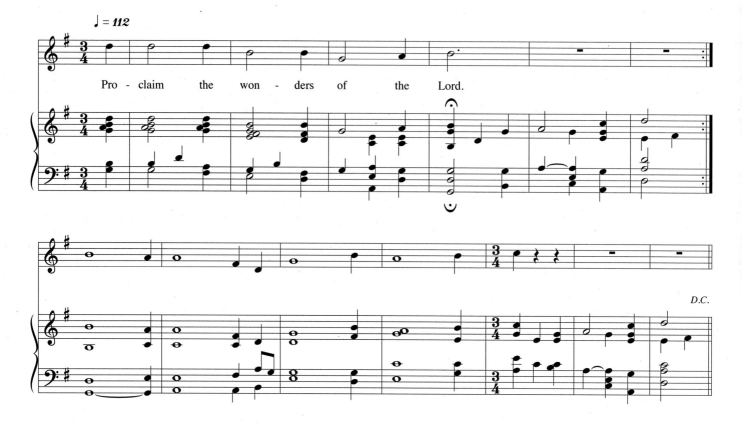

Pro - claim the won - ders of the Lord.

O Lord, you have searched me and · **known_me.**
You know when I sit down and when I · **rise** up**;**
you discern my thoughts from far a·-**way.**
You search out my path and my lying down, and are acquainted with all · **my** ways. R.

Even before a word is on my · **tongue,**
O Lord, you know it · **com**-pletely.
Such knowledge is too · **wonderful_for_me;**
it is so high that I cannot · **at**-tain_it. R.

Where can I go from your · **spirit?**
Or where can I flee from · **your** presence?
If I ascend to heaven, you are · **there;**
if I make my bed in Sheol, you · **are** there. R.

Even there your hand shall · **lead_me,**
and your right hand shall · **hold_me** fast.
How weighty to me are your thoughts, O · **God!**
How vast is · **the** sum_of_them! R.

Extended Vigil of Pentecost (4) – ABC

Psalm 139

Guitar

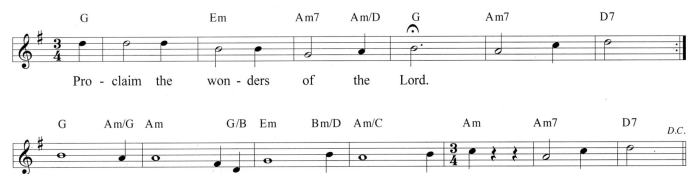

Pro - claim the won - ders of the Lord.

O Lord, you have searched me and · **known_me.**
You know when I sit down and when I · **rise** up;
you discern my thoughts from far a·-**way.**
You search out my path and my lying down, and are acquainted with all · **my** ways.

Even before a word is on my · **tongue,**
O Lord, you know it · **com**-pletely.
Such knowledge is too · **wonderful_for_me;**
it is so high that I cannot · **at**-tain_it. R.

Where can I go from your · **spirit?**
Or where can I flee from · **your** presence?
If I ascend to heaven, you are · **there;**
if I make my bed in Sheol, you · **are** there. R.

Even there your hand shall · **lead_me,**
and your right hand shall · **hold_me** fast.
How weighty to me are your thoughts, O · **God!**
How vast is · **the** sum_of_them! R.

C Instrument

B♭ Instrument

Extended Vigil of Pentecost (5) – ABC

Psalm 105

The Lord re - mem-bers his cov-e-nant for - ev - er.

D.C.

O give thanks to the Lord, call · **on_his** name,
make known his deeds a·-**mong_the** peoples.
Sing to him, sing · **praises** to him;
tell of all his · **wonderful** works. R.

Remember the wonderful works he · **has** done,
his miracles, and the judgments · **he** uttered,
O offspring of his · **ser**-vant Abraham,
children of Jacob, · **his** chosen_ones. R.

He is the Lord · **our** God;
his judgments are in all · **the** earth.
He is mindful of his · **covenant** for-ever,
the covenant that he made with Abraham, to Israel as an ever·-**lasting** covenant. R.

For he remembered his · **holy** promise,
and Abraham, · **his** servant,
that they might · **keep** his statutes
and observe · **his** laws. R.

Extended Vigil of Pentecost (5) – ABC

Psalm 105

Guitar

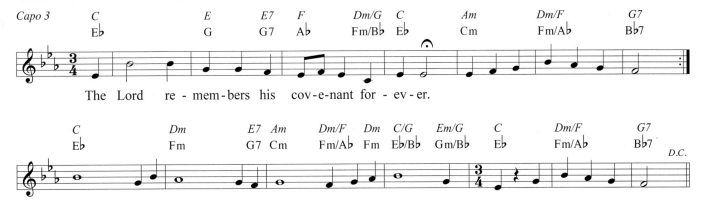

The Lord re - mem-bers his cov-e-nant for - ev - er.

O give thanks to the Lord, call · **on_his** name,
make known his deeds a-·-**mong_the** peoples.
Sing to him, sing · **praises** to him;
tell of all his · **wonderful** works. R.

Remember the wonderful works he · **has** done,
his miracles, and the judgments · **he** uttered,
O offspring of his · **ser**-vant Abraham,
children of Jacob, · **his** chosen_ones. R.

He is the Lord · **our** God;
his judgments are in all · **the** earth.
He is mindful of his · **covenant** for-ever,
the covenant that he made with Abraham, to Israel as an ever·-**lasting** covenant. R.

For he remembered his · **holy** promise,
and Abraham, · **his** servant,
that they might · **keep** his statutes
and observe · **his** laws. R.

C Instrument

B♭ Instrument

Extended Vigil of Pentecost (6) – ABC

Psalm 90

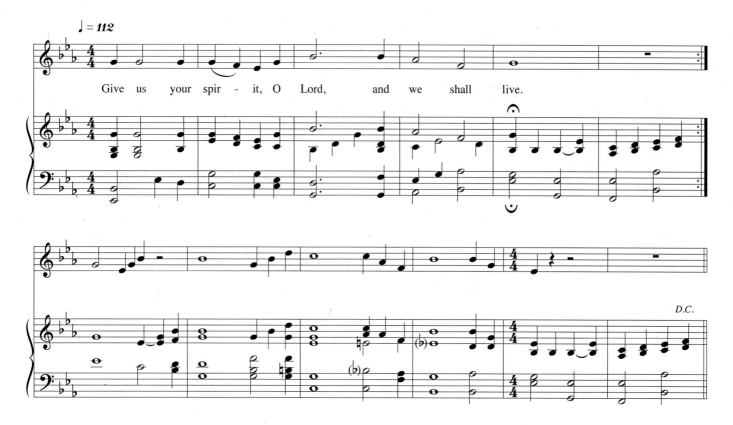

Lord, you have been our dwelling place in · **all** gene-rations.
Before the mountains · **were** brought forth,
or ever you had formed the · **earth_and** the world,
from everlasting to everlasting · **you** are God. R.

You turn man back to · **dust,** and say,
"Turn back, you · **children** of Adam
For a thousand years in your sight are like yesterday when · **it** is past,
or like a watch · **in** the night. R.

You sweep them away; they are · **like** a dream,
like grass that is renewed · **in** the morning;
in the morning it flourishes and · **is** re-newed;
in the evening it · **fades** and withers. R.

Satisfy us in the morning with your · **stead**-fast love,
so that we may rejoice and be glad · **all** our days.
Let your work be manifest · **to** your servants,
and your glorious power · **to** their children. R.

Extended Vigil of Pentecost (6) – ABC

Psalm 90

Guitar

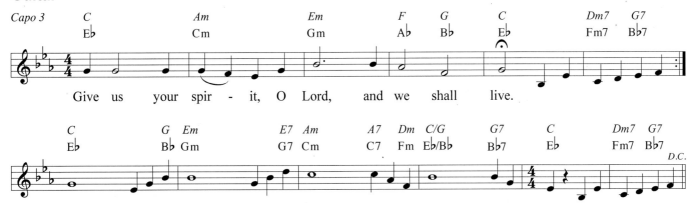

Give us your spir - it, O Lord, and we shall live.

Lord, you have been our dwelling place in · **all** gene-rations.
Before the mountains · **were** brought forth,
or ever you had formed the · **earth_and** the world,
from everlasting to everlasting · **you** are God. R.

You turn man back to · **dust,** and say,
"Turn back, you · **children** of Adam
For a thousand years in your sight are like yesterday when · **it** is past,
or like a watch · **in** the night. R.

You sweep them away; they are · **like** a dream,
like grass that is renewed · **in** the morning;
in the morning it flourishes and · **is** re-newed;
in the evening it · **fades** and withers. R.

Satisfy us in the morning with your · **stead**-fast love,
so that we may rejoice and be glad · **all** our days.
Let your work be manifest · **to** your servants,
and your glorious power · **to** their children. R.

C Instrument

B♭ Instrument

Extended Vigil of Pentecost (7) – ABC

Psalm 104

Bless the Lord, O · **my** soul.
O Lord my God, you are very · **great.**
You are clothed with · **honour** and majesty,
wrapped in light as with · **a** garment. R.

O Lord, how manifold are · **your** works!
In wisdom you have made them · **all;**
the earth is · **full_of** your creatures,
living things both small · **and** great. R.

These all look · **to** you
to give them their food in due · **season;**
when you give to them, they · **gather** it up;
when you open your hand, they are filled with · **good** things. R.

When you take away · **their** breath,
they die and return to their · **dust.**
When you send forth your spirit, they · **are** cre-ated;
and you renew the face of · **the** earth. R.

Extended Vigil of Pentecost (7) – ABC

Psalm 104

Guitar

Lord, send forth your Spir-it,___ and re - new the face of the earth.

Bless the Lord, O · **my** soul.
O Lord my God, you are very · **great.**
You are clothed with · **honour** and majesty,
wrapped in light as with · **a** garment. R.

O Lord, how manifold are · **your** works!
In wisdom you have made them : **all;**
the earth is · **full_of** your creatures,
living things both small · **and** great. R.

These all look · **to** you
to give them their food in due · **season;**
when you give to them, they · **gather** it up;
when you open your hand, they are filled with · **good** things. R.

When you take away · **their** breath,
they die and return to their · **dust.**
When you send forth your spirit, they · **are** cre-ated;
and you renew the face of · **the** earth. R.

C Instrument

B♭ Instrument

Pentecost Sunday – B

Psalm 104

Lord, send forth your Spir-it,_____ and re-new the face of the earth.

D.C.

Bless the Lord, O · **my** soul.
O Lord my God, you are very · **great.**
O Lord, how manifold · **are** your works!
The earth is full of · **your** creatures. R.

When you take away · **their** breath,
they die and return to their · **dust.**
When you send forth your spirit, they · **are** cre-ated;
and you renew the face of · **the** earth. R.

May the glory of the Lord endure · **for**-ever;
may the Lord rejoice in his · **works.**
May my meditation be · **pleasing** to him,
for I rejoice in · **the** Lord. R.

Pentecost Sunday – B

Psalm 104

Guitar

Lord, send forth your Spir-it,___ and re - new the face of the earth.

Bless the Lord, O · **my** soul.
O Lord my God, you are very · **great.**
O Lord, how manifold · **are** your works!
The earth is full of · **your** creatures. R.

When you take away · **their** breath,
they die and return to their · **dust.**
When you send forth your spirit, they · **are** cre-ated;
and you renew the face of · **the** earth. R.

May the glory of the Lord endure · **for-**ever;
may the Lord rejoice in his · **works.**
May my meditation be · **pleasing** to him,
for I rejoice in · **the** Lord. R.

C Instrument

B♭ Instrument

Solemnity of the Most Holy Trinity – B

Psalm 33

Bless-ed the peo-ple the Lord has chos-en as his her-it-age.

The word of the · **Lord** is upright,
and all his work is · **done** in faithfulness.
He loves · **righteousness** and justice;
the earth is full of the steadfast · **love_of** the Lord. R.

By the word of the Lord the · **heavens** were made,
and all their host by the breath · **of** his mouth.
For he spoke, and it · **came** to be;
he commanded, and · **it** stood firm. R.

Truly the eye of the Lord is on · **those** who fear_him,
on those who hope in his · **stead**-fast love,
to deliver their · **souls** from death,
and to keep them a·-**live** in famine. R.

Our soul waits · **for** the Lord;
he is our · **help** and shield.
Let your steadfast love, O Lord, · **be** up-on_us,
even as we · **hope** in you. R.

Solemnity of the Most Holy Trinity – B

May 27, 2018

Psalm 33

Guitar

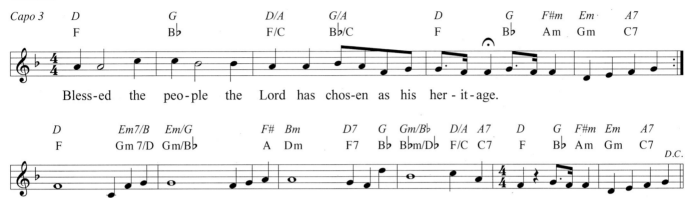

Bless-ed the peo-ple the Lord has chos-en as his her - it-age.

The word of the · **Lord** is upright,
and all his work is · **done** in faithfulness.
He loves · **righteousness** and justice;
the earth is full of the steadfast · **love_of** the Lord. R.

By the word of the Lord the · **heavens** were made,
and all their host by the breath · **of** his mouth.
For he spoke, and it · **came** to be;
he commanded, and · **it** stood firm. R.

Truly the eye of the Lord is on · **those** who fear_him,
on those who hope in his · **stead**-fast love,
to deliver their · **souls** from death,
and to keep them a·-**live** in famine. R.

Our soul waits · **for** the Lord;
he is our · **help** and shield.
Let your steadfast love, O Lord, · **be** up-on_us,
even as we · **hope** in you. R.

C Instrument

B♭ Instrument

141

Solemnity of the Most Holy Body and Blood of Christ – B

Psalm 116

I will lift up the cup of sal - va-tion, and call on the name of the Lord.

D.C.

What shall I return to the · **Lord**
for all his bounty to · **me?**
I will lift up the cup of sal·-**vation**
and call on the name · **of_the** Lord. R.

Precious in the sight of the · **Lord**
is the death of his · **faithful_ones.**
O Lord, I am your servant, the son of your · **serving_girl.**
You have loosed · **my** bonds. R.

I will offer to you a thanksgiving · **sacrifice**
and call on the name of the · **Lord.**
I will pay my vows to the · **Lord**
in the presence of all · **his** people. R.

Solemnity of the Most Holy Body and Blood of Christ – B

Psalm 116

Guitar

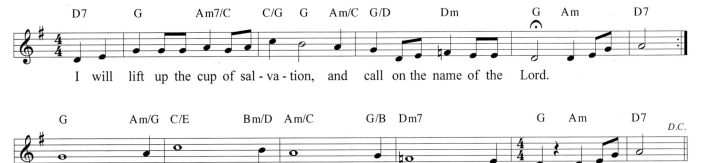

I will lift up the cup of sal - va - tion, and call on the name of the Lord.

What shall I return to the · **Lord**
for all his bounty to · **me?**
I will lift up the cup of sal·-**vation**
and call on the name · **of_the** Lord. R.

Precious in the sight of the · **Lord**
is the death of his · **faithful_ones.**
O Lord, I am your servant, the son of your · **serving_girl.**
You have loosed · **my** bonds. R.

I will offer to you a thanksgiving · **sacrifice**
and call on the name of the · **Lord.**
I will pay my vows to the · **Lord**
in the presence of all · **his** people. R.

C Instrument

B♭ Instrument

Solemnity of the Most Sacred Heart of Jesus – B

Isaiah 12

With joy you will draw wa-ter____ from the wells of sal - va-tion.

Surely God is my salvation; I will trust, and will not · **be** a-fraid,
for the Lord God is my strength and my might; he has be·-**come_my** sal-vation.
With joy · **you_will** draw water
from the wells · **of** sal-vation. R.

Give thanks · **to** the Lord,
call · **on** his name;
make known his deeds a·-**mong** the nations;
proclaim that his · **name_is** ex-alted. R.

Sing praises to the Lord, for he · **has** done gloriously;
let this be known in · **all** the earth.
Shout aloud and sing for joy, O · **roy**-al Zion,
for great in your midst is the Holy · **One** of Israel. R.

Solemnity of the Most Sacred Heart of Jesus – B

Isaiah 12

Guitar

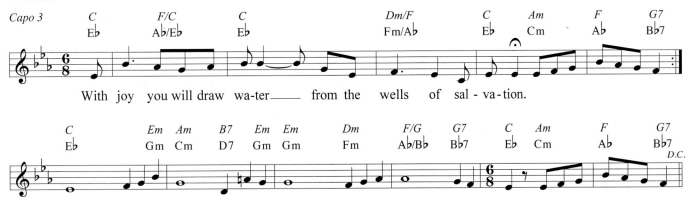

With joy you will draw wa-ter____ from the wells of sal - va-tion.

Surely God is my salvation; I will trust, and will not · **be** a-fraid,
for the Lord God is my strength and my might; he has be-·**come_my** sal-vation.
With joy · **you_will** draw water
from the wells · **of** sal-vation. R.

Give thanks · **to** the Lord,
call · **on** his name;
make known his deeds a-·**mong** the nations;
proclaim that his · **name_is** ex-alted. R.

Sing praises to the Lord, for he · **has** done gloriously;
let this be known in · **all** the earth.
Shout aloud and sing for joy, O · **roy**-al Zion,
for great in your midst is the Holy · **One** of Israel. R.

C Instrument

B♭ Instrument

Common Psalm for Ordinary Time

Psalm 19

Lord, you have the words of e - ter - nal life.

The law of the Lord is · **perfect,**
reviving the · **soul;**
the decrees of the Lord are · **sure,**
making · **wise** the simple. R.

The precepts of the Lord are · **right,**
rejoicing the · **heart;**
the commandment of the Lord is · **clear,**
en·-**lightening** the eyes. R.

The fear of the Lord is · **pure,**
enduring for·-**ever;**
the ordinances of the Lord are · **true**
and righteous · **al**-to-gether. R.

More to be desired are they than · **gold,**
even much fine · **gold;**
sweeter also than · **honey,**
and drippings · **of** the honeycomb. R.

146

Common Psalm for Ordinary Time

Psalm 19

Guitar

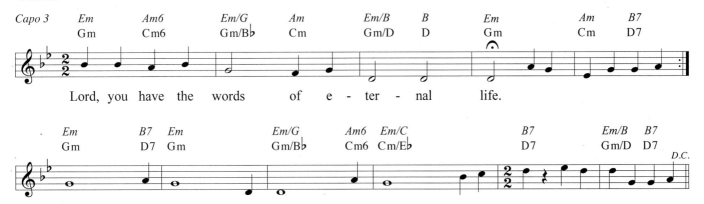

Lord, you have the words of e - ter - nal life.

The law of the Lord is · **perfect**,
reviving the · **soul;**
the decrees of the Lord are · **sure,**
making · **wise** the simple. R.

The precepts of the Lord are · **right,**
rejoicing the · **heart;**
the commandment of the Lord is · **clear,**
en-·**lightening** the eyes. R.

The fear of the Lord is · **pure,**
enduring for-·**ever;**
the ordinances of the Lord are · **true**
and righteous · **al**-to-gether. R.

More to be desired are they than · **gold,**
even much fine · **gold;**
sweeter also than · **honey,**
and drippings · **of** the honeycomb. R.

C Instrument

B♭ Instrument

Common Psalm for Ordinary Time

Psalm 27

The Lord is my light and my sal·-**vation;**
whom shall · **I** fear?
The Lord is the stronghold of my · **life;**
of whom shall I be · **a**-fraid? R.

One thing I asked of the Lord, that will I · **seek_after:**
to live in the house of the Lord all the days of · **my** life,
to behold the beauty of the · **Lord,**
and to inquire in · **his** temple. R.

I believe that I shall see the goodness of the · **Lord**
in the land of · **the** living.
Wait for the Lord; be · **strong,**
and let your heart take courage; wait · **for_the** Lord! R.

Common Psalm for Ordinary Time

Psalm 27

Guitar

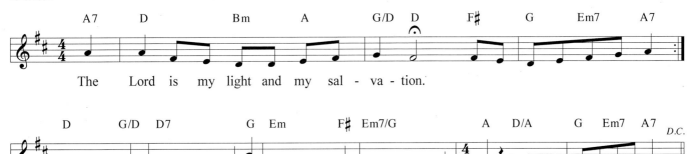

The Lord is my light and my sal - va - tion.

The Lord is my light and my sal·-**vation;**
whom shall · **I** fear?
The Lord is the stronghold of my · **life;**
of whom shall I be · **a**-fraid? R.

One thing I asked of the Lord, that will I · **seek_after:**
to live in the house of the Lord all the days of · **my** life,
to behold the beauty of the · **Lord,**
and to inquire in · **his** temple. R.

I believe that I shall see the goodness of the · **Lord**
in the land of · **the** living.
Wait for the Lord; be · **strong,**
and let your heart take courage; wait · **for_the** Lord! R.

C Instrument

B♭ Instrument

Common Psalm for Ordinary Time
Psalm 34

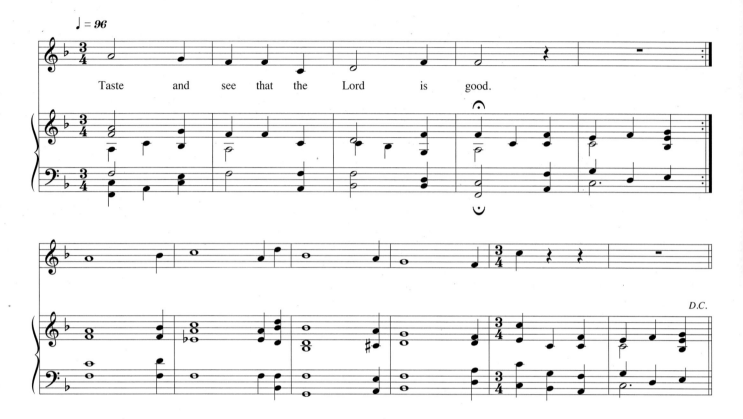

Taste and see that the Lord is good.

I will bless the Lord at all · **times;**
his praise shall continually be in · **my** mouth.
My soul makes its boast in the · **Lord;**
let the humble hear and · **be** glad. R.

O magnify the Lord with · **me,**
and let us exalt his name · **to**-gether.
I sought the Lord, and he · **answered_me,**
and delivered me from all · **my** fears. R.

Look to him, and be · **radiant;**
so your faces shall never · **be_a**-shamed.
The poor one called, and the Lord · **heard,**
and saved that person from ev·-**ery** trouble. R.

The Angel of the Lord en·-**camps**
around those who fear him, and · **de**-livers_them.
O taste and see that the Lord is · **good;**
blessed is the one who takes refuge · **in** him. R.

Common Psalm for Ordinary Time

Psalm 34

Guitar

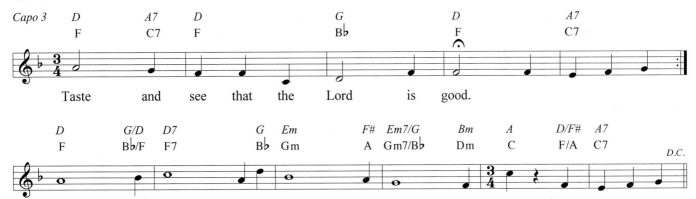

Taste and see that the Lord is good.

I will bless the Lord at all · **times;**
his praise shall continually be in · **my** mouth.
My soul makes its boast in the · **Lord;**
let the humble hear and · **be** glad. R.

O magnify the Lord with · **me,**
and let us exalt his name · **to**-gether.
I sought the Lord, and he · **answered_me,**
and delivered me from all · **my** fears. R.

Look to him, and be · **radiant;**
so your faces shall never · **be_a**-shamed.
The poor one called, and the Lord · **heard,**
and saved that person from ev·-**ery** trouble. R.

The Angel of the Lord en·-**camps**
around those who fear him, and · **de**-livers_them.
O taste and see that the Lord is · **good;**
blessed is the one who takes refuge · **in** him. R.

C Instrument

B♭ Instrument

151

Common Psalm for Ordinary Time

Psalm 63

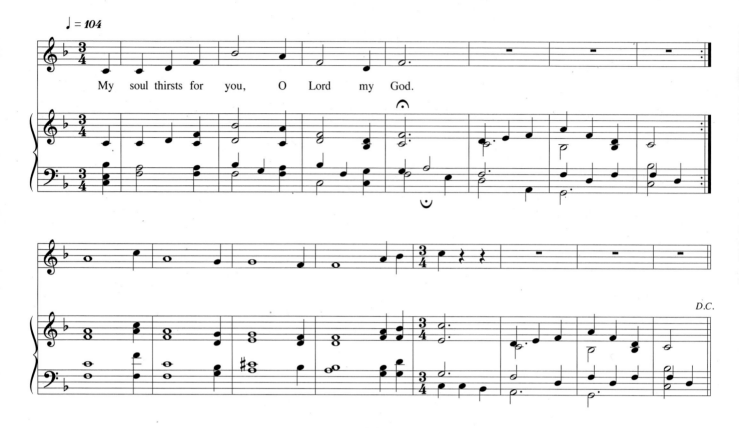

O God, you are my God, I · **seek_you,**
my soul · **thirsts_for_you;**
my flesh · **faints_for_you,**
as in a dry and weary land where there · **is** no water. R.

So I have looked upon you in the · **sanctuary,**
beholding your power and · **glory.**
Because your steadfast love is better than · **life,**
my · **lips** will praise_you. R.

So I will bless you as long as I · **live;**
I will lift up my hands and call on your · **name.**
My soul is satisfied as with a rich · **feast,**
and my mouth praises you with · **joy**-ful lips. R.

For you have been my · **help,**
and in the shadow of your wings I sing for · **joy.**
My soul · **clings_to_you;**
your right · **hand** up-holds_me. R.

Common Psalm for Ordinary Time

Psalm 63

Guitar

My soul thirsts for you, O Lord my God.

O God, you are my God, I · **seek_you,**
my soul · **thirsts_for_you;**
my flesh · **faints_for_you,**
as in a dry and weary land where there · **is** no water. R.

So I have looked upon you in the · **sanctuary,**
beholding your power and · **glory.**
Because your steadfast love is better than · **life,**
my · **lips** will praise_you. R.

So I will bless you as long as I · **live;**
I will lift up my hands and call on your · **name.**
My soul is satisfied as with a rich · **feast,**
and my mouth praises you with · **joy**-ful lips. R.

For you have been my · **help,**
and in the shadow of your wings I sing for · **joy.**
My soul · **clings_to_you;**
your right · **hand** up-holds_me. R.

C Instrument

B♭ Instrument

Common Psalm for Ordinary Time

Psalm 95

O come, let us sing to · **the** Lord;
let us make a joyful noise to the rock of our · **sal**-vation!
Let us come into his presence with · **thanks**-giving;
let us make a joyful noise to him with songs · **of** praise! R.

O come, let us worship and · **bow** down,
let us kneel before the Lord, · **our** Maker!
For he is our God, and we are the people of · **his** pasture,
and the sheep of · **his** hand. R.

O that today you would listen to · **his** voice!
Do not harden your hearts, as at Meribah, as on the day at Massah in · **the** wilderness,
when your ancestors tested me, and put me to · **the** proof,
though they had seen · **my** work. R.

Common Psalm for Ordinary Time

Psalm 95

Guitar

O that to-day you would lis-ten to the voice of the Lord. Do not hard-en your hearts!

O come, let us sing to · **the** Lord;
let us make a joyful noise to the rock of our · **sal**-vation!
Let us come into his presence with · **thanks**-giving;
let us make a joyful noise to him with songs · **of** praise! R.

O come, let us worship and · **bow** down,
let us kneel before the Lord, · **our** Maker!
For he is our God, and we are the people of · **his** pasture,
and the sheep of · **his** hand. R.

O that today you would listen to · **his** voice!
Do not harden your hearts, as at Meribah, as on the day at Massah in · **the** wilderness,
when your ancestors tested me, and put me to · **the** proof,
though they had seen · **my** work. R.

C Instrument

B♭ Instrument

Common Psalm for Ordinary Time

Psalm 100

Make a joyful noise to the Lord, all · **the** earth.
Worship the Lord with · **gladness;**
come into his presence · **with** singing. R.

Know that the Lord · **is** God.
It is he that made us, and we are · **his;**
we are his people, and the sheep of · **his** pasture. R.

For the Lord · **is** good;
his steadfast love endures for·-**ever,**
and his faithfulness to all · **gene**-rations. R.

Common Psalm for Ordinary Time

Psalm 100

Guitar

We are his peo-ple: the sheep of his pas - ture.

Make a joyful noise to the Lord, all · **the** earth.
Worship the Lord with · **gladness;**
come into his presence · **with** singing. R.

Know that the Lord · **is** God.
It is he that made us, and we are · **his;**
we are his people, and the sheep of · **his** pasture. R.

For the Lord · **is** good;
his steadfast love endures for·-**ever,**
and his faithfulness to all · **gene**-rations. R.

C Instrument

B♭ Instrument

Common Psalm for Ordinary Time

Psalm 103

Bless the Lord, O my · **soul,**
and all that is within me, bless his · **holy** name.
Bless the Lord, O my · **soul,**
and do not forget all · **his** benefits. R.

It is the Lord who forgives all your in-·**iquity,**
who heals all your · **dis**-eases,
who redeems your life from the · **Pit,**
who crowns you with steadfast love · **and** mercy. R.

The Lord is merciful and · **gracious,**
slow to anger and abounding in stead-·**fast** love.
He does not deal with us according to our · **sins,**
nor repay us according to our · **in**-iquities. R.

As far as the east is from the · **west,**
so far he removes our transgressions · **from** us.
As a father has compassion for his · **children,**
so the Lord has compassion for those · **who** fear_him. R.

Common Psalm for Ordinary Time

Psalm 103

Guitar

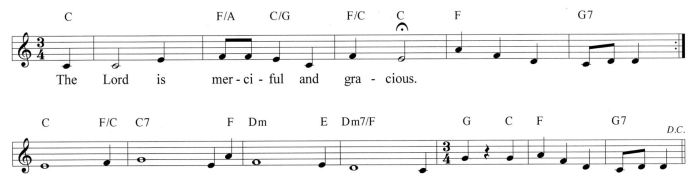

The Lord is mer - ci - ful and gra - cious.

Bless the Lord, O my · **soul,**
and all that is within me, bless his · **holy** name.
Bless the Lord, O my · **soul,**
and do not forget all · **his** benefits. R.

It is the Lord who forgives all your in·-**iquity,**
who heals all your · **dis**-eases,
who redeems your life from the · **Pit,**
who crowns you with steadfast love · **and** mercy. R.

The Lord is merciful and · **gracious,**
slow to anger and abounding in stead·-**fast** love.
He does not deal with us according to our · **sins,**
nor repay us according to our · **in**-iquities. R.

As far as the east is from the · **west,**
so far he removes our transgressions · **from** us.
As a father has compassion for his · **children,**
so the Lord has compassion for those · **who** fear_him. R.

C Instrument

B♭ Instrument

Common Psalm for Ordinary Time

Psalm 145

I will bless your name for ev - er, my King and my God.

I will extol you, my God and · **King,**
and bless your name forever and · **ever.**
Every day I will · **bless_you,**
and praise your name forever · **and** ever. R.

The Lord is gracious and · **merciful,**
slow to anger and abounding in steadfast · **love.**
The Lord is good to · **all,**
and his compassion is over all that he · **has** made. R.

All your works shall give thanks to you, O · **Lord,**
and all your faithful shall · **bless_you.**
They shall speak of the glory of your · **kingdom,**
and tell of · **your** power. R.

The Lord is faithful in all his · **words,**
and gracious in all his · **deeds.**
The Lord upholds all who are · **falling,**
and raises up all who are · **bowed** down. R.

Common Psalm for Ordinary Time

Psalm 145

Guitar

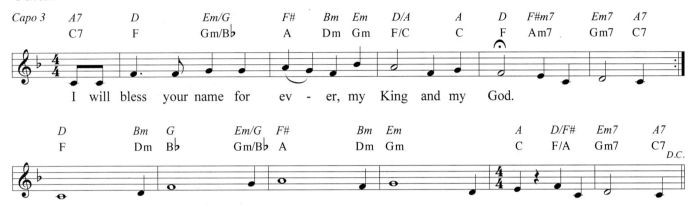

I will bless your name for ev - er, my King and my God.

I will extol you, my God and · **King,**
and bless your name forever and · **ever.**
Every day I will · **bless_you,**
and praise your name forever · **and** ever. R.

The Lord is gracious and · **merciful,**
slow to anger and abounding in steadfast · **love.**
The Lord is good to · **all,**
and his compassion is over all that he · **has** made. R.

All your works shall give thanks to you, O · **Lord,**
and all your faithful shall · **bless_you.**
They shall speak of the glory of your · **kingdom,**
and tell of · **your** power. R.

The Lord is faithful in all his · **words,**
and gracious in all his · **deeds.**
The Lord upholds all who are · **falling,**
and raises up all who are · **bowed** down. R.

C Instrument

B♭ Instrument

161

Common Psalm for the Last Weeks of Ordinary Time

Psalm 122

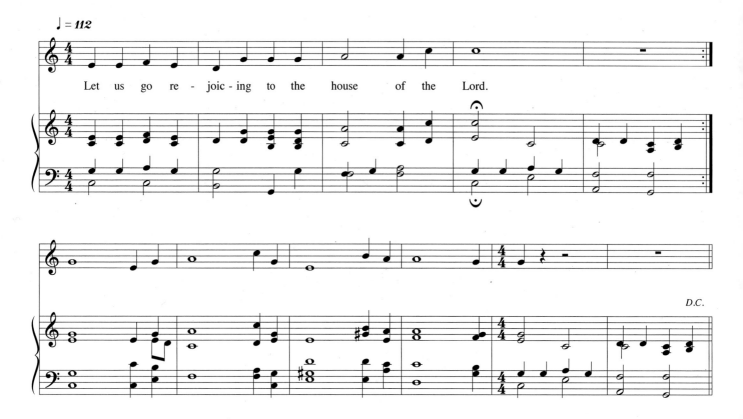

Let us go re-joic-ing to the house of the Lord.

I was glad when they said · **to** me,
"Let us go to the house of · **the** Lord!"
Our feet · **are** standing
within your gates, O · **Je**-rusalem. R.

Jerusalem—built as · **a** city
that is bound firmly · **to**-gether.
To it the tribes · **go** up,
the tribes · **of_the** Lord. R.

As was decreed · **for** Israel,
to give thanks to the name of · **the** Lord.
For there the thrones for judgment · **were_set** up,
the thrones of the · **house_of** David. R.

Pray for the peace of · **Je**-rusalem:
"May they prosper · **who** love_you.
Peace be within · **your** walls,
and security within · **your** towers." R.

For the sake of my relatives · **and** friends
I will say, "Peace be · **with**-in_you."
For the sake of the house of the Lord · **our** God,
I will seek · **your** good. R.

Common Psalm for the Last Weeks of Ordinary Time

Psalm 122

Guitar

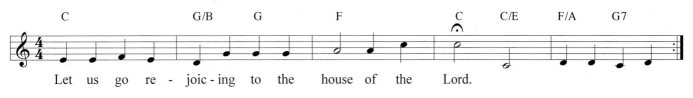

Let us go re - joic - ing to the house of the Lord.

I was glad when they said · **to** me,
"Let us go to the house of · **the** Lord!"
Our feet · **are** standing
within your gates, O · **Je**-rusalem. R.

Jerusalem—built as · **a** city
that is bound firmly · **to**-gether.
To it the tribes · **go** up,
the tribes · **of_the** Lord. R.

As was decreed · **for** Israel,
to give thanks to the name of · **the** Lord.
For there the thrones for judgment · **were_set** up,
the thrones of the · **house_of** David. R.

Pray for the peace of · **Je**-rusalem:
"May they prosper · **who** love_you.
Peace be within · **your** walls,
and security within · **your** towers." R.

For the sake of my relatives · **and** friends
I will say, "Peace be · **with**-in_you."
For the sake of the house of the Lord · **our** God,
I will seek · **your** good. R.

C Instrument

B♭ Instrument

Second Sunday in Ordinary Time – B

Psalm 40

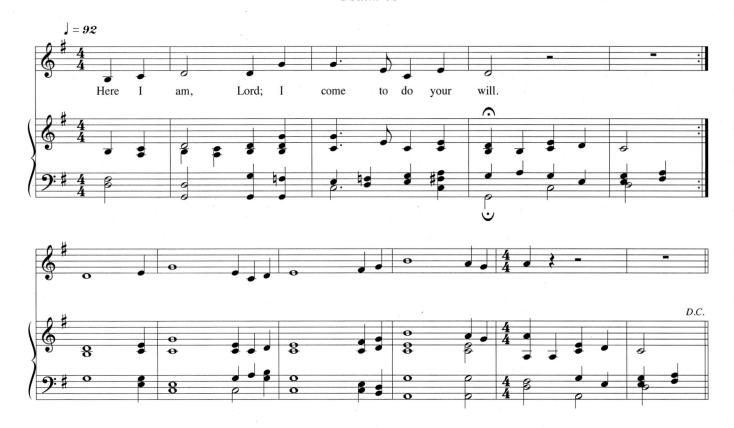

I waited patiently for the · **Lord;**
he inclined to me and · **heard** my cry.
He put a new song in · **my** mouth,
a song of praise · **to** our God. R.

Sacrifice and offering you do not de·-**sire,**
but you have given me an · **o-**pen ear.
Burnt offering · **and** sin_offering
you have · **not** re-quired. R.

Then I said, "Here I · **am;**
in the scroll of the book it is · **written** of me.
I delight to do your will, O · **my** God;
your law is with·-**in** my heart." R.

I have told the glad news of de·-**liverance**
in the great · **con-**gre-gation;
see, I have not restrained · **my** lips,
as you · **know,** O Lord. R.

Second Sunday in Ordinary Time – B

Psalm 40

Guitar

Here I am, Lord; I come to do your will.

I waited patiently for the · **Lord;**
he inclined to me and · **heard** my cry.
He put a new song in · **my** mouth,
a song of praise · **to** our God. R.

Sacrifice and offering you do not de·-**sire,**
but you have given me an · **o**-pen ear.
Burnt offering · **and** sin_offering
you have · **not** re-quired. R.

Then I said, "Here I · **am;**
in the scroll of the book it is · **written** of me.
I delight to do your will, O · **my** God;
your law is with·-**in** my heart." R.

I have told the glad news of de·-**liverance**
in the great · **con**-gre-gation;
see, I have not restrained · **my** lips,
as you · **know,** O Lord. R.

C Instrument

B♭ Instrument

Third Sunday in Ordinary Time – B

Psalm 25

Lord, make me know your ways.

Make me to know your ways, O · **Lord;**
teach me · **your** paths.
Lead me in your truth, and · **teach_me,**
for you are the God of my · **sal**-vation. R.

Be mindful of your mercy, O Lord, and of your steadfast · **love,**
for they have been from · **of** old.
According to your steadfast love re-·**member_me,**
for the sake of your goodness, · **O** Lord! R.

Good and upright is the · **Lord;**
therefore he instructs sinners in · **the** way.
He leads the humble in what is · **right,**
and teaches the humble · **his** way. R.

Third Sunday in Ordinary Time – B

Psalm 25

Jan 21, 2018

Guitar

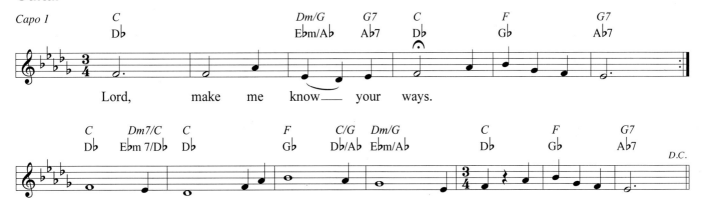

Lord, make me know your ways.

Make me to know your ways, O · **Lord;**
teach me · **your** paths.
Lead me in your truth, and · **teach_me,**
for you are the God of my · **sal**-vation. R.

Be mindful of your mercy, O Lord, and of your steadfast · **love,**
for they have been from · **of** old.
According to your steadfast love re·-**member_me,**
for the sake of your goodness, · **O** Lord! R.

Good and upright is the · **Lord;**
therefore he instructs sinners in · **the** way.
He leads the humble in what is · **right,**
and teaches the humble · **his** way. R.

C Instrument

B♭ Instrument

Fourth Sunday in Ordinary Time – B

Psalm 95

O that to-day you would lis-ten to the voice of the Lord. Do not hard-en your hearts!

O come, let us sing to · **the** Lord;
let us make a joyful noise to the rock of our · **sal**-vation!
Let us come into his presence with · **thanks**-giving;
let us make a joyful noise to him with songs · **of** praise! R.

O come, let us worship and · **bow** down,
let us kneel before the Lord, · **our** Maker!
For he is our God, and we are the people of · **his** pasture,
and the sheep of · **his** hand. R.

O that today you would listen to · **his** voice!
Do not harden your hearts, as at Meribah, as on the day at Massah in · **the** wilderness,
when your ancestors tested me, and put me to · **the** proof,
though they had seen · **my** work. R.

Fourth Sunday in Ordinary Time – B

Psalm 95

Guitar

O that to-day you would lis-ten to the voice of the Lord. Do not hard-en your hearts!

O come, let us sing to · **the** Lord;
let us make a joyful noise to the rock of our · **sal**-vation!
Let us come into his presence with · **thanks**-giving;
let us make a joyful noise to him with songs · **of** praise! R.

O come, let us worship and · **bow** down,
let us kneel before the Lord, · **our** Maker!
For he is our God, and we are the people of · **his** pasture,
and the sheep of · **his** hand. R.

O that today you would listen to · **his** voice!
Do not harden your hearts, as at Meribah, as on the day at Massah in · **the** wilderness,
when your ancestors tested me, and put me to · **the** proof,
though they had seen · **my** work. R.

C Instrument

B♭ Instrument

Fifth Sunday in Ordinary Time – B

Psalm 147

D.C.

How good it is to sing praises · **to** our God;
for he is gracious, and a song of · **praise** is fitting.
The Lord builds · **up** Je-rusalem;
he gathers the · **outcasts** of Israel. R.

The Lord heals the · **bro**-ken-hearted,
and binds · **up** their wounds.
He determines the · **number** of_the stars;
he gives to all of · **them** their names. R.

Great is our Lord, and a-·**bundant** in power;
his understanding · **is_be**-yond measure.
The Lord lifts · **up** the downtrodden;
he casts the wicked · **to** the ground. R.

Fifth Sunday in Ordinary Time – B

Psalm 147

Guitar

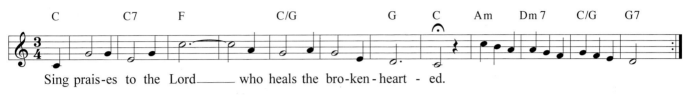

Sing prais-es to the Lord_____ who heals the bro-ken-heart - ed.

How good it is to sing praises · **to** our God;
for he is gracious, and a song of · **praise** is fitting.
The Lord builds · **up** Je-rusalem;
he gathers the · **outcasts** of Israel. R.

The Lord heals the · **bro**-ken-hearted,
and binds · **up** their wounds.
He determines the · **number** of_the stars;
he gives to all of · **them** their names. R.

Great is our Lord, and a·-**bundant** in power;
his understanding · **is_be**-yond measure.
The Lord lifts · **up** the downtrodden;
he casts the wicked · **to** the ground. R.

C Instrument

B♭ Instrument

Sixth Sunday in Ordinary Time – B

Psalm 32

You are my ref-uge, Lord; with de-liv-er-ance you sur-round me.

Blessed is the one whose transgression is for·-**given,**
whose sin is · **covered.**
Blessed is the one to whom the Lord imputes no in·-**iquity,**
and in whose spirit there is no de·-**ceit.** R.

I acknowledged my sin to · **you,**
and I did not hide my in·-**iquity;**
I said, "I will confess my transgressions to the · **Lord,"**
and you forgave the guilt of my · **sin.** R.

1 - Be glad in the Lord and rejoice, O · **righteous,**
4 - and shout for joy, all you upright in · **heart.** R.

Sixth Sunday in Ordinary Time – B

Psalm 32

Guitar

You are my ref-uge, Lord; with de - liv - er-ance you sur - round me.

Blessed is the one whose transgression is for·-**given,**
whose sin is · **covered.**
Blessed is the one to whom the Lord imputes no in·-**iquity,**
and in whose spirit there is no de·-**ceit.** R.

I acknowledged my sin to · **you,**
and I did not hide my in-**iquity;**
I said, "I will confess my transgressions to the · **Lord,"**
and you forgave the guilt of my · **sin.** R.

1 - Be glad in the Lord and rejoice, O · **righteous,**
4 - and shout for joy, all you upright in · **heart.** R.

C Instrument

B♭ Instrument

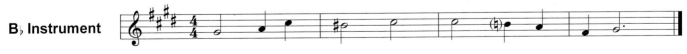

Seventh Sunday in Ordinary Time – B

Psalm 41

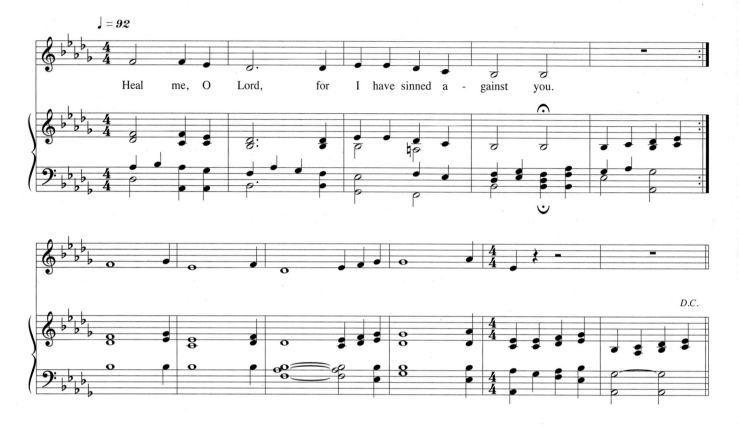

Heal me, O Lord, for I have sinned a-gainst you.

1 - Blessed is the one who considers the · **poor;**
2 - the Lord delivers them in the day of · **trouble.**
1 - The Lord protects them and keeps them a·-**live,**
2 - makes them happy in the · **land,**
3 - and does not · **give** them up
4 - to the will of · **their** enemies. R.

The Lord sustains that person on their · **sickbed;**
in their illness you heal all their in·-**firmities.**
As for me, I said, "O Lord, be · **gracious** to me;
heal me, for I have sinned · **a**-gainst_you." R.

But you have upheld me because of my in·-**tegrity,**
and set me in your presence for·-**ever.**
Blessed be the Lord, the · **God** of Israel,
from everlasting to · **ever**-lasting. R.

Seventh Sunday in Ordinary Time – B

Psalm 41

Guitar

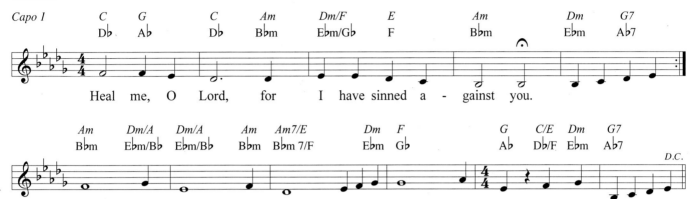

Heal me, O Lord, for I have sinned a - gainst you.

1 - Blessed is the one who considers the · **poor;**
2 - the Lord delivers them in the day of · **trouble.**
1 - The Lord protects them and keeps them a·-**live,**
2 - makes them happy in the · **land,**
3 - and does not · **give** them up
4 - to the will of · **their** enemies. R.

The Lord sustains that person on their · **sickbed;**
in their illness you heal all their in·-**firmities.**
As for me, I said, "O Lord, be · **gracious** to me;
heal me, for I have sinned · **a**-gainst_you." R.

But you have upheld me because of my in·-**tegrity,**
and set me in your presence for·-**ever.**
Blessed be the Lord, the · **God** of Israel,
from everlasting to · **ever**-lasting. R.

C Instrument

B♭ Instrument

Eighth Sunday in Ordinary Time – B
Psalm 103

Bless the Lord, O my · **soul,**
and all that is within me, bless his · **holy** name.
Bless the Lord, O my · **soul,**
and do not forget all · **his** benefits. R.

It is the Lord who forgives all your in·-**iquity,**
who heals all your · **dis-**eases,
who redeems your life from the · **Pit,**
who crowns you with steadfast love · **and** mercy. R.

The Lord is merciful and · **gracious,**
slow to anger and abounding in stead·-**fast** love.
He does not deal with us according to our · **sins,**
nor repay us according to our · **in-**iquities. R.

As far as the east is from the · **west,**
so far he removes our transgressions · **from** us.
As a father has compassion for his · **children,**
so the Lord has compassion for those · **who** fear_him. R.

Eighth Sunday in Ordinary Time – B

Psalm 103

Guitar

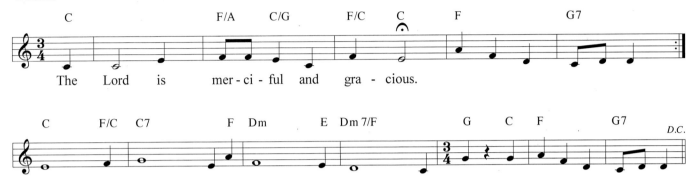

The Lord is mer-ci-ful and gra-cious.

Bless the Lord, O my · **soul,**
and all that is within me, bless his · **holy** name.
Bless the Lord, O my · **soul,**
and do not forget all · **his** benefits. R.

It is the Lord who forgives all your in·-**iquity,**
who heals all your · **dis**-eases,
who redeems your life from the · **Pit,**
who crowns you with steadfast love · **and** mercy. R.

The Lord is merciful and · **gracious,**
slow to anger and abounding·in stead·-**fast** love.
He does not deal with us according to our · **sins,**
nor repay us according to our · **in**-iquities. R.

As far as the east is from the · **west,**
so far he removes our transgressions · **from** us.
As a father has compassion for his · **children,**
so the Lord has compassion for those · **who** fear_him. R.

C Instrument

B♭ Instrument

Ninth Sunday in Ordinary Time – B

Psalm 81

Sing a - loud to God our strength.

Raise a song, sound the · **tambour**-ine,
the sweet lyre with · **the** harp.
Blow the trumpet at the · **new** moon,
at the full moon, on our · **festal** day. R.

For it is a statute · **for** Israel,
an ordinance of the God · **of** Jacob.
He made it a decree · **in** Joseph,
when he went out over the land · **of** Egypt. R.

I hear a voice I had · **not** known:
"I relieved your shoulder · **of_the** burden;
your hands were freed · **from_the** basket.
In distress you called, and · **I** rescued_you." R.

There shall be no strange god · **a**-mong_you;
you shall not bow to a · **foreign** god.
I am the Lord · **your** God,
who brought you up out of the land · **of** Egypt. R.

Ninth Sunday in Ordinary Time – B

Psalm 81

Guitar

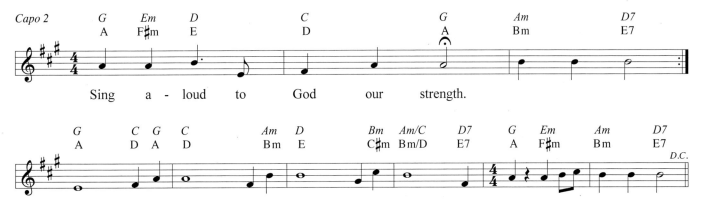

Sing a - loud to God our strength.

Raise a song, sound the · **tambour**-ine,
the sweet lyre with · **the** harp.
Blow the trumpet at the · **new** moon,
at the full moon, on our · **festal** day. R.

For it is a statute · **for** Israel,
an ordinance of the God · **of** Jacob.
He made it a decree · **in** Joseph,
when he went out over the land · **of** Egypt. R.

I hear a voice I had · **not** known:
"I relieved your shoulder · **of_the** burden;
your hands were freed · **from_the** basket.
In distress you called, and · **I** rescued_you." R.

There shall be no strange god · **a**-mong_you;
you shall not bow to a · **foreign** god.
I am the Lord · **your** God,
who brought you up out of the land · **of** Egypt. R.

C Instrument

B♭ Instrument

Tenth Sunday in Ordinary Time – B

Psalm 130

With the Lord there is stead-fast love, and great pow'r to re-deem.

Out of the depths I cry to you, O · **Lord.**
Lord, hear · **my** voice!
Let your ears be at·-**tentive**
to the voice of my sup·-**pli**-cations! R.

If you, O Lord, should mark in·-**iquities,**
Lord, who · **could** stand?
But there is forgiveness with · **you,**
so that you may be · **re**-vered. R.

I wait for the · **Lord,**
my soul waits, and in his word · **I** hope;
my soul waits for the · **Lord**
more than watchmen for · **the** morning. R.

For with the Lord there is steadfast · **love,**
and with him is great power to · **re**-deem.
It is he who will redeem · **Israel**
from all its · **in**-iquities. R.

Tenth Sunday in Ordinary Time – B

June 10, 2018

Psalm 130

Guitar

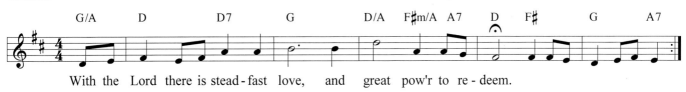

With the Lord there is stead-fast love, and great pow'r to re-deem.

Out of the depths I cry to you, O · **Lord.**
Lord, hear · **my** voice!
Let your ears be at·-**tentive**
to the voice of my sup·-**pli**-cations! R.

If you, O Lord, should mark in·-**iquities,**
Lord, who · **could** stand?
But there is forgiveness with · **you,**
so that you may be · **re**-vered. R.

I wait for the · **Lord,**
my soul waits, and in his word · **I** hope;
my soul waits for the · **Lord**
more than watchmen for · **the** morning. R.

For with the Lord there is steadfast · **love,**
and with him is great power to · **re**-deem.
It is he who will redeem · **Israel**
from all its · **in**-iquities. R.

C Instrument

B♭ Instrument

181

Eleventh Sunday in Ordinary Time – B

Psalm 92

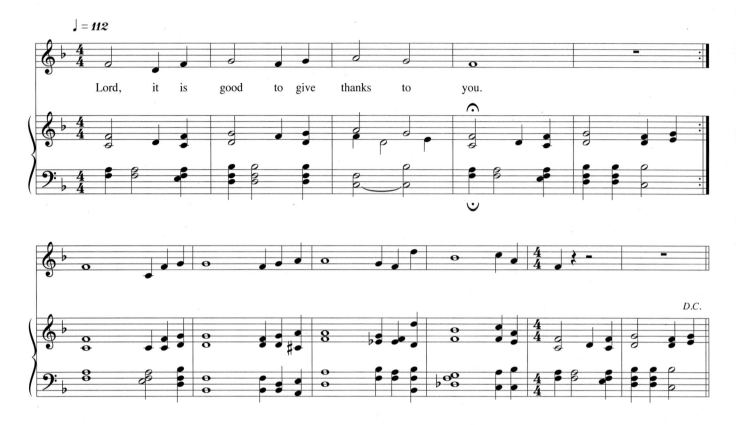

Lord, it is good to give thanks to you.

It is good to give thanks · **to** the Lord,
to sing praises to your name, · **O** Most High;
to declare your steadfast love · **in** the morning,
and your · **faithfulness** by night. R.

The righteous flourish · **like** the palm_tree,
and grow like a · **cedar** in Lebanon.
They are planted in the house · **of** the Lord;
they flourish in the · **courts_of** our God. R.

In old age they · **still_pro**-duce fruit;
they are always green and · **full** of sap,
showing that the · **Lord** is upright;
he is my rock, and there is no un·-**righteousness** in him. R.

Eleventh Sunday in Ordinary Time – B

Psalm 92

Guitar

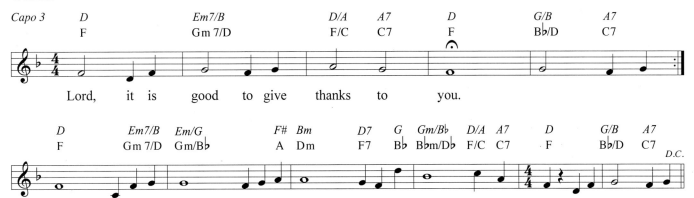

Lord, it is good to give thanks to you.

It is good to give thanks · **to** the Lord,
to sing praises to your name, · **O** Most High;
to declare your steadfast love · **in** the morning,
and your · **faithfulness** by night. R.

The righteous flourish · **like** the palm_tree,
and grow like a · **cedar** in Lebanon.
They are planted in the house · **of** the Lord;
they flourish in the · **courts_of** our God. R.

In old age they · **still_pro**-duce fruit;
they are always green and · **full** of sap,
showing that the · **Lord** is upright;
he is my rock, and there is no un-·**righteousness** in him. R.

C Instrument

B♭ Instrument

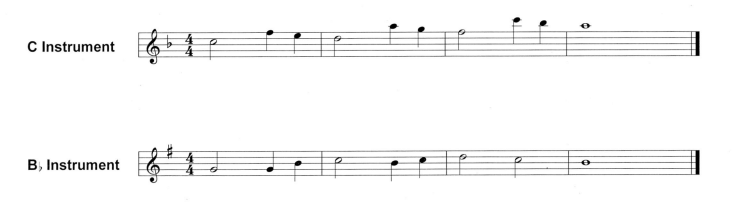

Twelfth Sunday in Ordinary Time – B

Psalm 107

Give thanks to the Lord;_____ his stead-fast love en-dures for-ev-er.

Some went down to the sea in · **ships,**
doing business on the mighty · **waters;**
they saw the deeds of the · **Lord,**
his wondrous works in the · **deep.** R.

For he commanded and raised the stormy · **wind,**
which lifted up the waves of the · **sea.**
They mounted up to heaven and they went down to the · **depths;**
their courage melted away in their cal·-**amity.** R.

Then they cried to the Lord in their · **trouble,**
and he brought them out from their dis·-**tress;**
he made the storm be · **still,**
and the waves of the sea were · **hushed.** R.

Then they were glad when it grew · **calm,**
and he brought them to their desired · **haven.**
Let them thank the Lord for his steadfast · **love,**
for his wonderful works to the children of · **Adam.** R.

Twelfth Sunday in Ordinary Time – B
Psalm 107

Guitar

Give thanks to the Lord;— his stead-fast love en-dures for-ev-er.

Some went down to the sea in · **ships,**
doing business on the mighty · **waters;**
they saw the deeds of the · **Lord,**
his wondrous works in the · **deep.** R.

For he commanded and raised the stormy · **wind,**
which lifted up the waves of the · **sea.**
They mounted up to heaven and they went down to the · **depths;**
their courage melted away in their cal·-**amity.** R.

Then they cried to the Lord in their · **trouble,**
and he brought them out from their dis·-**tress;**
he made the storm be · **still,**
and the waves of the sea were · **hushed.** R.

Then they were glad when it grew · **calm,**
and he brought them to their desired · **haven.**
Let them thank the Lord for his steadfast · **love,**
for his wonderful works to the children of · **Adam.** R.

C Instrument

B♭ Instrument

Thirteenth Sunday in Ordinary Time – B

Psalm 30

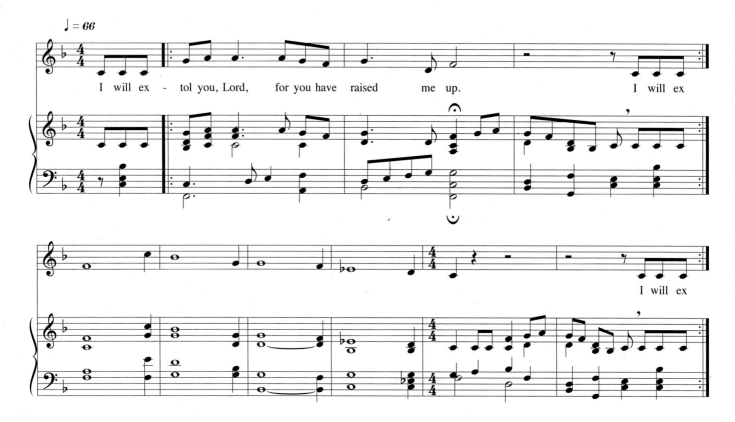

I will extol you, O Lord, for you have drawn me · **up,**
and did not let my foes rejoice · **over_me.**
O Lord, you brought up my soul from · **Sheol,**
restored me to life from among those gone down · **to_the** Pit. R.

Sing praises to the Lord, O you his · **faithful_ones,**
and give thanks to his holy · **name.**
For his anger is but for a moment; his favour is for a · **lifetime.**
Weeping may linger for the night, but joy comes · **with_the** morning. R.

Hear, O Lord, and be gracious to · **me!**
O Lord, be my · **helper!**
You have turned my mourning into · **dancing.**
O Lord my God, I will give thanks to you · **for**-ever. R.

Thirteenth Sunday in Ordinary Time – B

Psalm 30

Guitar

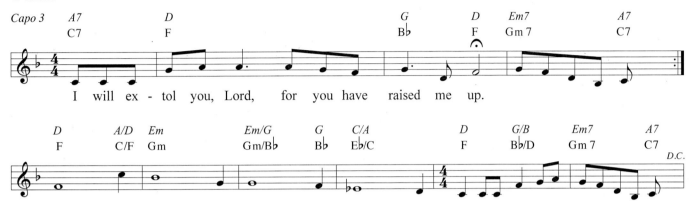

I will ex-tol you, Lord, for you have raised me up.

I will extol you, O Lord, for you have drawn me · **up,**
and did not let my foes rejoice · **over_me.**
O Lord, you brought up my soul from · **Sheol,**
restored me to life from among those gone down · **to_the** Pit. R.

Sing praises to the Lord, O you his · **faithful_ones,**
and give thanks to his holy · **name.**
For his anger is but for a moment; his favour is for a · **lifetime.**
Weeping may linger for the night, but joy comes · **with_the** morning. R.

Hear, O Lord, and be gracious to · **me!**
O Lord, be my · **helper!**
You have turned my mourning into · **dancing.**
O Lord my God, I will give thanks to you · **for**-ever. R.

C Instrument

B♭ Instrument

Fourteenth Sunday in Ordinary Time – B

Psalm 123

To you I lift up my · **eyes**—
O you who are enthroned in · **the** heavens—
as the eyes of · **servants**
look to the hand of · **their** master. R.

As the eyes of a · **maid**
to the hand of · **her** mistress,
so our eyes look to the Lord our · **God,**
until he has mercy · **up**-on_us. R.

Have mercy upon us, O Lord, have · **mercy,**
for we have had more than enough of · **con**-tempt.
Our soul has had more than its fill of the · **scorn**
of those who are at ease, of the contempt of · **the** proud. R.

Fourteenth Sunday in Ordinary Time – B

Psalm 123

Guitar

Our eyes look to the Lord, un-til he has mer-cy up-on us.

To you I lift up my · **eyes**—
O you who are enthroned in · **the** heavens—
as the eyes of · **servants**
look to the hand of · **their** master. R.

As the eyes of a · **maid**
to the hand of · **her** mistress,
so our eyes look to the Lord our · **God,**
until he has mercy · **up**-on_us. R.

Have mercy upon us, O Lord, have · **mercy,**
for we have had more than enough of · **con**-tempt.
Our soul has had more than its fill of the · **scorn**
of those who are at ease, of the contempt of · **the** proud. R.

C Instrument

B♭ Instrument

Fifteenth Sunday in Ordinary Time – B

Psalm 85

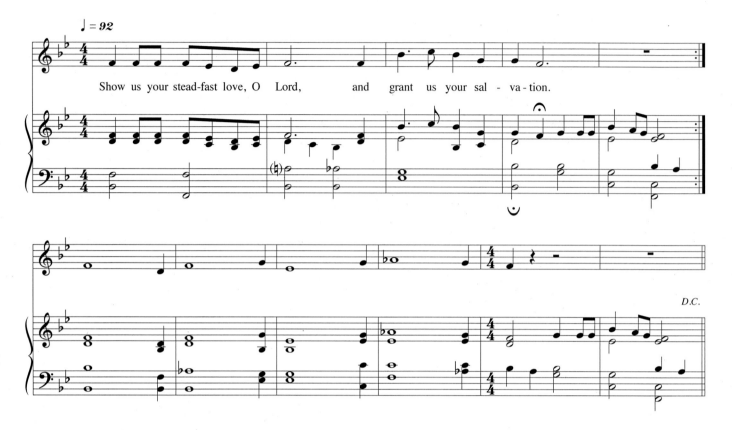

Show us your stead-fast love, O Lord, and grant us your sal - va - tion.

Let me hear what God the Lord will · **speak,**
for he will speak peace to his · **people.**
Surely his salvation is at hand for those who · **fear_him,**
that his glory may dwell · **in_our** land. R.

Steadfast love and faithfulness will · **meet;**
righteousness and peace will · **kiss_each_other.**
Faithfulness will spring up from the · **ground,**
and righteousness will look down · **from_the** sky. R.

The Lord will give what is · **good,**
and our land will yield its · **increase.**
Righteousness will go be·-**fore_him,**
and will make a path · **for_his** steps. R.

190

Fifteenth Sunday in Ordinary Time – B

Psalm 85

Guitar

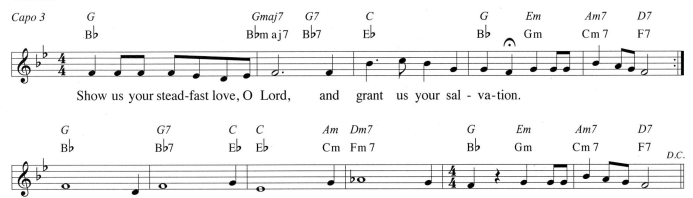

Show us your stead-fast love, O Lord, and grant us your sal - va-tion.

Let me hear what God the Lord will · **speak,**
for he will speak peace to his · **people.**
Surely his salvation is at hand for those who · **fear_him,**
that his glory may dwell · **in_our** land. R.

Steadfast love and faithfulness will · **meet;**
righteousness and peace will · **kiss_each_other.**
Faithfulness will spring up from the · **ground,**
and righteousness will look down · **from_the** sky. R.

The Lord will give what is · **good,**
and our land will yield its · **increase.**
Righteousness will go be-·**fore_him,**
and will make a path · **for_his** steps. R.

C Instrument

B♭ Instrument

Sixteenth Sunday in Ordinary Time – B

Psalm 23

The Lord is my shepherd, I shall · **not** want.
He makes me lie down in · **green** pastures;
he leads me be·-**side** still waters;
he re·-**stores** my soul. R.

He leads me in right paths for his · **name's** sake.
Even though I walk through the darkest valley, I fear · **no** evil;
for · **you** are with_me;
your rod and your · **staff**—they comfort_me. R.

You prepare a table · **be**-fore_me
in the presence · **of_my** enemies;
you anoint my · **head** with oil;
my · **cup** over-flows. R.

Surely goodness and mercy · **shall** follow_me
all the days of · **my** life,
and I shall dwell in the · **house_of** the Lord
my · **whole** life long. R.

Sixteenth Sunday in Ordinary Time – B

Psalm 23

Guitar

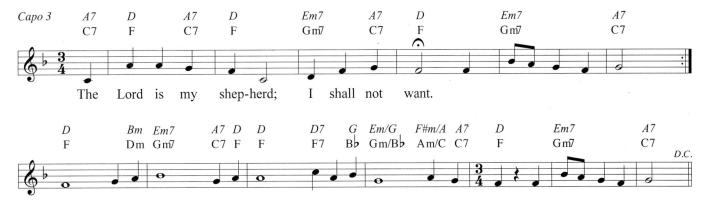

The Lord is my shep-herd; I shall not want.

The Lord is my shepherd, I shall · **not** want.
He makes me lie down in · **green** pastures;
he leads me be·-**side** still waters;
he re·-**stores** my soul. R.

He leads me in right paths for his · **name's** sake.
Even though I walk through the darkest valley, I fear · **no** evil;
for · **you** are with_me;
your rod and your · **staff**—they comfort_me. R.

You prepare a table · **be**-fore_me
in the presence · **of_my** enemies;
you anoint my · **head** with oil;
my · **cup** over-flows. R.

Surely goodness and mercy · **shall** follow_me
all the days of · **my** life,
and I shall dwell in the · **house_of** the Lord
my · **whole** life long. R.

C Instrument

B♭ Instrument

193

Seventeenth Sunday in Ordinary Time – B

Psalm 145

You o-pen your hand to feed us, Lord; you sat-is-fy all our needs.

All your works shall give thanks to you, O · **Lord,**
and all your faithful shall · **bless_you.**
They shall speak of the glory of your · **kingdom,**
and tell of · **your** power. R.

The eyes of all look to · **you,**
and you give them their food in due · **season.**
You open your · **hand,**
satisfying the desire of every · **living** thing. R.

The Lord is just in all his · **ways,**
and kind in all his · **doings.**
The Lord is near to all who · **call_on_him,**
to all who call on him · **in** truth. R.

Seventeenth Sunday in Ordinary Time – B

Psalm 145

Guitar

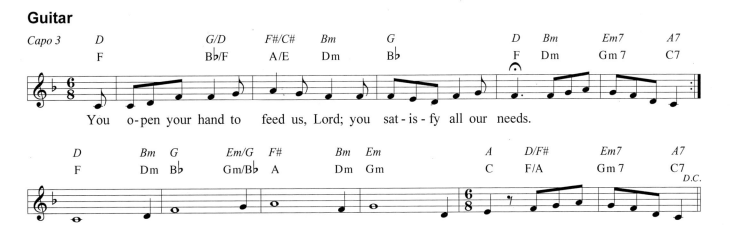

You o-pen your hand to feed us, Lord; you sat-is-fy all our needs.

All your works shall give thanks to you, O · **Lord,**
and all your faithful shall · **bless_you.**
They shall speak of the glory of your · **kingdom,**
and tell of · **your** power. R.

The eyes of all look to · **you,**
and you give them their food in due · **season.**
You open your · **hand,**
satisfying the desire of every · **living** thing. R.

The Lord is just in all his · **ways,**
and kind in all his · **doings.**
The Lord is near to all who · **call_on_him,**
to all who call on him · **in** truth. R.

C Instrument

B♭ Instrument

Eighteenth Sunday in Ordinary Time – B

Psalm 78

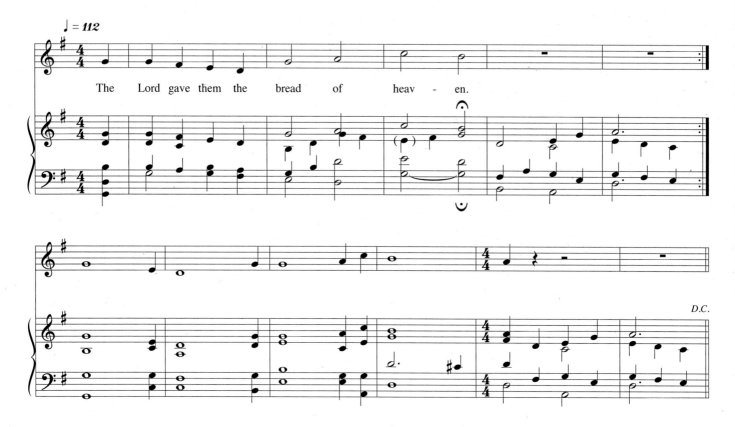

The Lord gave them the bread of heav - en.

D.C.

Things that we have heard and known, that our ancestors have · **told_us,**
we will not · **hide;**
we will tell to the coming generation the glorious deeds of the Lord, and · **hi**s might,
and the wonders that he has · **done.** R.

He commanded the skies a·-**bove,**
and opened the doors of · **heaven;**
he rained down on them manna · **to** eat,
and gave them the bread of · **heaven.** R.

Man ate of the bread of · **Angels;**
he sent them food in a·-**bundance.**
And he brought them to his · **holy** hill,
to the mountain that his right hand had · **won.** R.

Eighteenth Sunday in Ordinary Time – B

Psalm 78

Guitar

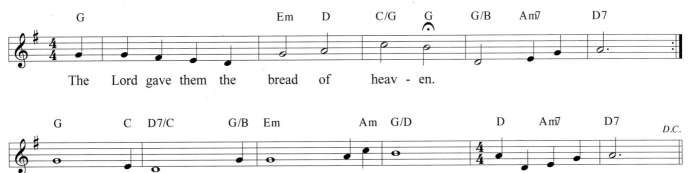

The Lord gave them the bread of heav - en.

Things that we have heard and known, that our ancestors have · **told_us,**
we will not · **hide;**
we will tell to the coming generation the glorious deeds of the Lord, and · **hi**s might,
and the wonders that he has · **done.** R.

He commanded the skies a·-**bove,**
and opened the doors of · **heaven;**
he rained down on them manna · **to** eat,
and gave them the bread of · **heaven.** R.

Man ate of the bread of · **Angels;**
he sent them food in a·-**bundance.**
And he brought them to his · **holy** hill,
to the mountain that his right hand had · **won.** R.

C Instrument

B♭ Instrument

Nineteenth Sunday in Ordinary Time – B

Psalm 34

I will bless the Lord at all · **times;**
his praise shall continually be in · **my** mouth.
My soul makes its boast in the · **Lord;**
let the humble hear and · **be** glad. R.

O magnify the Lord with · **me,**
and let us exalt his name · **to**-gether.
I sought the Lord, and he · **answered_me,**
and delivered me from all · **my** fears. R.

Look to him, and be · **radiant;**
so your faces shall never · **be_a**-shamed.
The poor one called, and the Lord · **heard,**
and saved that person from ev·-**ery** trouble. R.

The Angel of the Lord en·-**camps**
around those who fear him, and · **de**-livers_them.
O taste and see that the Lord is · **good;**
blessed is the one who takes refuge · **in** him. R.

Nineteenth Sunday in Ordinary Time – B

Psalm 34

Guitar

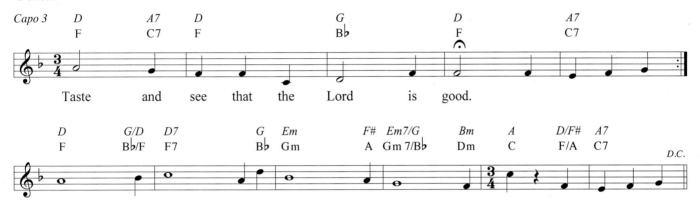

Taste and see that the Lord is good.

I will bless the Lord at all · **times;**
his praise shall continually be in · **my** mouth.
My soul makes its boast in the · **Lord;**
let the humble hear and · **be** glad. R.

O magnify the Lord with · **me,**
and let us exalt his name · **to**-gether.
I sought the Lord, and he · **answered_me,**
and delivered me from all · **my** fears. R.

Look to him, and be · **radiant;**
so your faces shall never · **be_a**-shamed.
The poor one called, and the Lord · **heard,**
and saved that person from ev·-**ery** trouble. R.

The Angel of the Lord en·-**camps**
around those who fear him, and · **de**-livers_them.
O taste and see that the Lord is · **good;**
blessed is the one who takes refuge · **in** him. R.

C Instrument

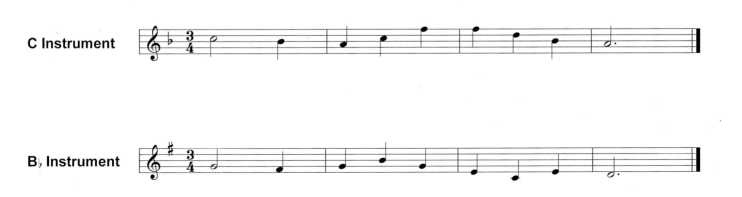

B♭ Instrument

Twentieth Sunday in Ordinary Time – B

Psalm 34

Taste and see that the Lord is good.

I will bless the Lord at all · **times;**
his praise shall continually be in · **my** mouth.
My soul makes its boast in the · **Lord;**
let the humble hear and · **be** glad. R.

O fear the Lord, you his · **holy_ones,**
for those who fear him have · **no** want.
The young lions suffer want and · **hunger,**
but those who seek the Lord lack no · **good** thing. R.

Come, O children, · **listen_to_me;**
I will teach you the fear of · **the** Lord.
Which of you desires · **life,**
and covets many days to en·-**joy** good? R.

Keep your tongue from · **evil,**
and your lips from speaking · **de**-ceit.
Depart from evil, and do · **good;**
seek peace, and · **pur**-sue_it. R.

Twentieth Sunday in Ordinary Time – B
Psalm 34

Guitar

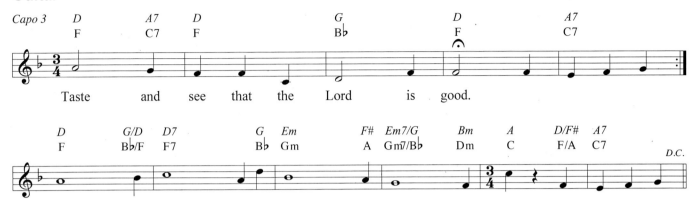

Taste and see that the Lord is good.

I will bless the Lord at all · **times;**
his praise shall continually be in · **my** mouth.
My soul makes its boast in the · **Lord;**
let the humble hear and · **be** glad. R.

O fear the Lord, you his · **holy_ones,**
for those who fear him have · **no** want.
The young lions suffer want and · **hunger,**
but those who seek the Lord lack no · **good** thing. R.

Come, O children, · **listen_to_me;**
I will teach you the fear of · **the** Lord.
Which of you desires · **life,**
and covets many days to en·-**joy** good? R.

Keep your tongue from · **evil,**
and your lips from speaking · **de**-ceit.
Depart from evil, and do · **good;**
seek peace, and · **pur**-sue_it. R.

C Instrument

B♭ Instrument

Twenty-first Sunday in Ordinary Time – B

Psalm 34

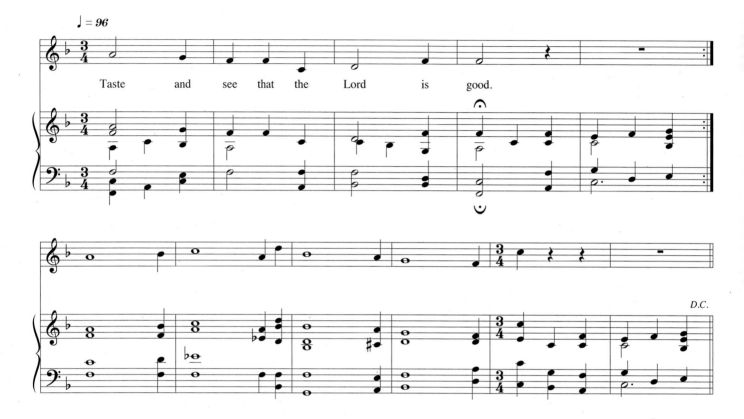

Taste and see that the Lord is good.

I will bless the Lord at all · **times;**
his praise shall continually be in · **my** mouth.
My soul makes its boast in the · **Lord;**
let the humble hear and · **be** glad. R.

The eyes of the Lord are on the · **righteous,**
and his ears are open · **to_their** cry.
The face of the Lord is against · **evildoers,**
to cut off the remembrance of them · **from_the** earth. R.

When the righteous cry for help, the Lord · **hears,**
and rescues them from all · **their** troubles.
The Lord is near to the broken·-**hearted,**
and saves the crushed · **in** spirit. R.

Many are the afflictions of the · **righteous_one,**
but the Lord rescues him from · **them** all.
He keeps all his · **bones;**
not one of them will · **be** broken. R.

Evil brings death to the · **wicked,**
and those who hate the righteous will be · **con**-demned.
The Lord redeems the life of his · **servants;**
none of those who take refuge in him will be · **con**-demned. R.

Twenty-first Sunday in Ordinary Time – B

Psalm 34

Guitar

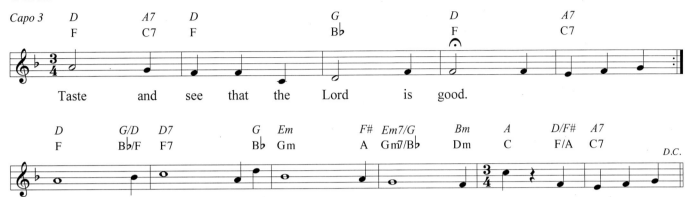

Taste and see that the Lord is good.

I will bless the Lord at all · **times;**
his praise shall continually be in · **my** mouth.
My soul makes its boast in the · **Lord;**
let the humble hear and · **be** glad. R.

The eyes of the Lord are on the · **righteous,**
and his ears are open · **to_their** cry.
The face of the Lord is against · **evildoers,**
to cut off the remembrance of them · **from_the** earth. R.

When the righteous cry for help, the Lord · **hears,**
and rescues them from all · **their** troubles.
The Lord is near to the broken·-**hearted,**
and saves the crushed · **in** spirit. R.

Many are the afflictions of the · **righteous_one,**
but the Lord rescues him from · **them** all.
He keeps all his · **bones;**
not one of them will · **be** broken. R.

Evil brings death to the · **wicked,**
and those who hate the righteous will be · **con-**demned.
The Lord redeems the life of his · **servants;**
none of those who take refuge in him will be · **con-**demned. R.

C Instrument

B♭ Instrument

Twenty-second Sunday in Ordinary Time – B

Psalm 15

O Lord, who may a-bide in your tent?

Whoever walks · **blamelessly,**
and does what is · **right,**
and speaks the truth from their · **heart;**
whoever does not slander · **with_their** tongue. R.

Whoever does no evil to a · **friend,**
nor takes up a reproach against a · **neighbour;**
in whose eyes the wicked one is de·-**spised,**
but who honours those who fear · **the** Lord. R.

Whoever stands by their oath even to their · **hurt;**
who does not lend money at · **interest,**
and does not take a bribe against the · **innocent.**
One who does these things shall never · **be** moved. R.

Twenty-second Sunday in Ordinary Time – B

Psalm 15

September 2, 2018

Guitar

O   Lord,   who may a - bide   in your   tent?

Whoever walks · **blamelessly,**
and does what is · **right,**
and speaks the truth from their · **heart;**
whoever does not slander · **with_their** tongue. R.

Whoever does no evil to a · **friend,**
nor takes up a reproach against a · **neighbour;**
in whose eyes the wicked one is de·-**spised,**
but who honours those who fear · **the** Lord. R.

Whoever stands by their oath even to their · **hurt;**
who does not lend money at · **interest,**
and does not take a bribe against the · **innocent.**
One who does these things shall never · **be** moved. R.

C Instrument

B♭ Instrument

Twenty-third Sunday in Ordinary Time – B

Psalm 146

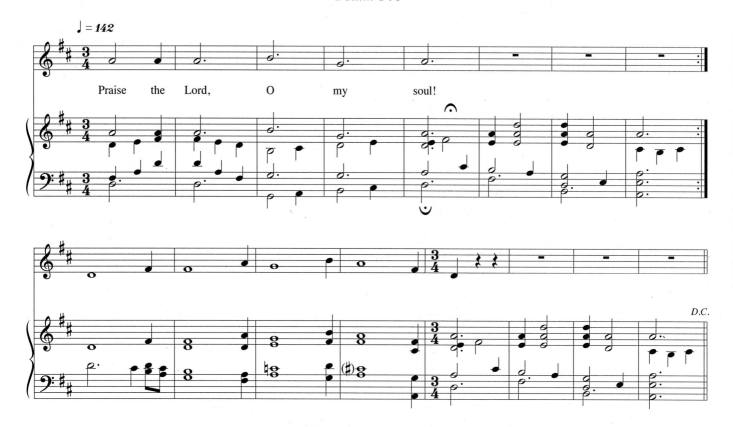

Praise the Lord, O my soul!

It is the Lord who keeps faith for·-**ever,**
who executes justice for the op·-**pressed;**
who gives food to the · **hungry.**
The Lord sets the · **prisoners** free. R.

The Lord opens the eyes of the · **blind**
and lifts up those who are bowed · **down;**
the Lord loves the · **righteous**
and watches over · **the** strangers. R.

The Lord upholds the orphan and the · **widow,**
but the way of the wicked he brings to · **ruin.**
The Lord will reign for·-**ever,**
your God, O Zion, for all · **gener**-ations. R.

Twenty-third Sunday in Ordinary Time – B

Psalm 146

Guitar

Praise the Lord, O my soul!

It is the Lord who keeps faith for·-**ever,**
who executes justice for the op·-**pressed;**
who gives food to the · **hungry.**
The Lord sets the · **prisoners** free. R.

The Lord opens the eyes of the · **blind**
and lifts up those who are bowed · **down;**
the Lord loves the · **righteous**
and watches over · **the** strangers. R.

The Lord upholds the orphan and the · **widow,**
but the way of the wicked he brings to · **ruin.**
The Lord will reign for·-**ever,**
your God, O Zion, for all · **gener**-ations. R.

C Instrument

B♭ Instrument

Twenty-fourth Sunday in Ordinary Time – B

Psalm 116

I love the Lord, because he has · **heard**
my voice and my · **suppli**-cations.
Because he inclined his ear to · **me,**
therefore I will call on him as long as · **I** live. R.

The snares of death encompassed me; the pangs of Sheol laid · **hold_on_me;**
I suffered distress · **and** anguish.
Then I called on the name of the · **Lord:**
"O Lord, I pray, save · **my** life!" R.

Gracious is the Lord, and · **righteous;**
our God · **is** merciful.
The Lord protects the · **simple;**
when I was brought low, · **he** saved_me. R.

For you have delivered my soul from · **death,**
my eyes from tears, my feet · **from** stumbling.
I will walk before the · **Lord**
in the land of · **the** living. R.

Twenty-fourth Sunday in Ordinary Time – B

Psalm 116

September 16, 2018

Guitar

I will walk be - fore the Lord, in the land of the liv - ing.

I love the Lord, because he has · **heard**
my voice and my · **suppli**-cations.
Because he inclined his ear to · **me,**
therefore I will call on him as long as · **I** live. R.

The snares of death encompassed me; the pangs of Sheol laid · **hold_on_me;**
I suffered distress · **and** anguish.
Then I called on the name of the · **Lord:**
"O Lord, I pray, save · **my** life!" R.

Gracious is the Lord, and · **righteous;**
our God · **is** merciful.
The Lord protects the · **simple;**
when I was brought low, · **he** saved_me. R.

For you have delivered my soul from · **death,**
my eyes from tears, my feet · **from** stumbling.
I will walk before the · **Lord**
in the land of · **the** living. R.

C Instrument

B♭ Instrument

Twenty-fifth Sunday in Ordinary Time – B

Psalm 54

The Lord up - holds my life.

Save me, O God, by your · **name,**
and vindicate me by · **your** might.
Hear my prayer, O · **God;**
give ear to the words of · **my** mouth. R.

1 - For the insolent have risen a-·**gainst_me,**
2 - the ruthless seek · **my** life;
4 - they do not set God · **be**-fore_them. R.

But surely, God is my · **helper;**
the Lord is the upholder of · **my** life.
With a freewill offering I will · **sacrifice_to_you;**
I will give thanks to your name, for · **it_is** good. R.

Twenty-fifth Sunday in Ordinary Time – B

Psalm 54

Guitar

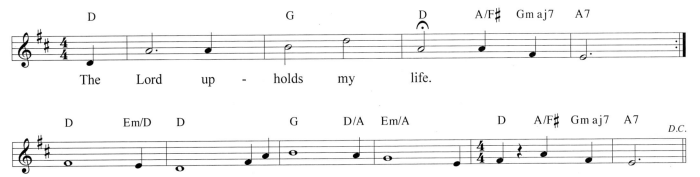

The Lord up - holds my life.

Save me, O God, by your · **name,**
and vindicate me by · **your** might.
Hear my prayer, O · **God;**
give ear to the words of · **my** mouth. R.

1 - For the insolent have risen a-**gainst_me,**
2 - the ruthless seek · **my** life;
4 - they do not set God · **be**-fore_them. R.

But surely, God is my · **helper;**
the Lord is the upholder of · **my** life.
With a freewill offering I will · **sacrifice_to_you;**
I will give thanks to your name, for · **it_is** good. R.

C Instrument

B♭ Instrument

Twenty-sixth Sunday in Ordinary Time – B

Psalm 19

The pre-cepts of the Lord are right, and give joy to the heart.

The law of the Lord is · **perfect,**
reviving the · **soul;**
the decrees of the Lord are · **sure,**
making wise · **the** simple. R.

The fear of the Lord is · **pure,**
enduring for·-**ever;**
the ordinances of the Lord are · **true**
and righteous · **alto**-gether. R.

By them is your servant · **warned;**
in keeping them there is great re·-**ward.**
But who can detect unmindful · **errors?**
Clear me from · **hidden** faults. R.

Keep back your servant also from the · **insolent;**
do not let them have dominion · **over_me.**
Then I shall be · **blameless,**
and innocent of · **great_trans**-gression. R.

Twenty-sixth Sunday in Ordinary Time – B

Psalm 19

Guitar

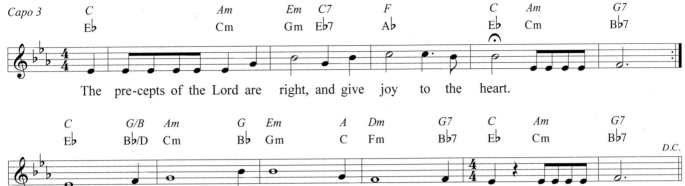

The pre-cepts of the Lord are right, and give joy to the heart.

The law of the Lord is · **perfect,**
reviving the · **soul;**
the decrees of the Lord are · **sure,**
making wise · **the** simple. R.

The fear of the Lord is · **pure,**
enduring for·-**ever;**
the ordinances of the Lord are · **true**
and righteous · **alto**-gether. R.

By them is your servant · **warned;**
in keeping them there is great re·-**ward.**
But who can detect unmindful · **errors?**
Clear me from · **hidden** faults. R.

Keep back your servant also from the · **insolent;**
do not let them have dominion · **over_me.**
Then I shall be · **blameless,**
and innocent of · **great_trans**-gression. R.

C Instrument

B♭ Instrument

Twenty-seventh Sunday in Ordinary Time – B

Psalm 128

May the Lord bless us all the days of our lives.

Blessed is everyone who fears · **the** Lord,
who walks in · **his** ways.
You shall eat the fruit of the labour of · **your** hands;
you shall be happy, and it shall go well · **with** you. R.

Your wife will be like a fruit·-**ful** vine
within · **your** house;
your children will be · **like** olive_shoots
around · **your** table. R.

Thus shall the man be blessed who fears · **the** Lord.
The Lord bless you · **from** Zion.
May you see the prosperity of · **Je**-rusalem
all the days of · **your** life. R.

Twenty-seventh Sunday in Ordinary Time – B

Psalm 128

Guitar

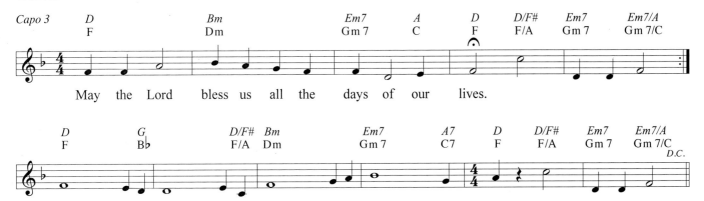

May the Lord bless us all the days of our lives.

Blessed is everyone who fears · **the** Lord,
who walks in · **his** ways.
You shall eat the fruit of the labour of · **your** hands;
you shall be happy, and it shall go well · **with** you. R.

Your wife will be like a fruit·-**ful** vine
within · **your** house;
your children will be · **like** olive_shoots
around · **your** table. R.

Thus shall the man be blessed who fears · **the** Lord.
The Lord bless you · **from** Zion.
May you see the prosperity of · **Je**-rusalem
all the days of · **your** life. R.

C Instrument

B♭ Instrument

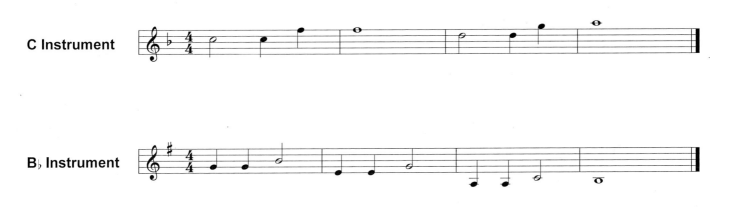

Twenty-eighth Sunday in Ordinary Time – B

Psalm 90

Fill us— with your love, O Lord, that we may re-joice and be glad.

Teach us to count our · **days**
that we may gain a wise · **heart.**
Turn, O Lord! How · **long?**
Have compassion · **on_your** servants! R.

Satisfy us in the morning with your steadfast · **love,**
so that we may rejoice and be glad all our · **days.**
Make us glad as many days as you have af-·**flicted_us,**
and as many years as we have · **seen** evil. R.

Let your work be manifest to your · **servants,**
and your glorious power to their · **children.**
Let the favour of the Lord our God be up-·**on_us,**
and prosper for us the work of · **our** hands. R.

Twenty-eighth Sunday in Ordinary Time – B

Psalm 90

Guitar

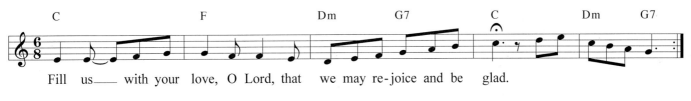

Fill us—— with your love, O Lord, that we may re-joice and be glad.

Teach us to count our · **days**
that we may gain a wise · **heart.**
Turn, O Lord! How · **long?**
Have compassion · **on_your** servants! R.

Satisfy us in the morning with your steadfast · **love,**
so that we may rejoice and be glad all our · **days.**
Make us glad as many days as you have af·-**flicted_us,**
and as many years as we have · **seen** evil. R.

Let your work be manifest to your · **servants,**
and your glorious power to their · **children.**
Let the favour of the Lord our God be up·-**on_us,**
and prosper for us the work of · **our** hands. R.

C Instrument

B♭ Instrument

Twenty-ninth Sunday in Ordinary Time – B

Psalm 33

Let your love be up-on us, Lord, e-ven as we hope in you.

The word of the Lord is · **upright,**
and all his work is done in · **faithfulness.**
He loves righteousness and · **justice;**
the earth is full of the steadfast love of the · **Lord.** R.

Truly the eye of the Lord is on those who · **fear_him,**
on those who hope in his steadfast · **love,**
to deliver their soul from · **death,**
and to keep them alive in · **famine.** R.

Our soul waits for the · **Lord;**
he is our help and · **shield.**
Let your steadfast love, O Lord, be up·-**on_us,**
even as we hope in · **you.** R.

Twenty-ninth Sunday in Ordinary Time – B

Psalm 33

Guitar

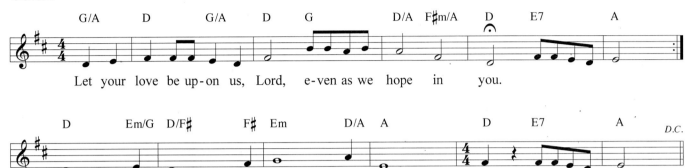

Let your love be up-on us, Lord, e-ven as we hope in you.

The word of the Lord is · **upright,**
and all his work is done in · **faithfulness.**
He loves righteousness and · **justice;**
the earth is full of the steadfast love of the · **Lord.** R.

Truly the eye of the Lord is on those who · **fear_him,**
on those who hope in his steadfast · **love,**
to deliver their soul from · **death,**
and to keep them alive in · **famine.** R.

Our soul waits for the · **Lord;**
he is our help and · **shield.**
Let your steadfast love, O Lord, be up·-**on_us,**
even as we hope in · **you.** R.

C Instrument

B♭ Instrument

Thirtieth Sunday in Ordinary Time – B

Psalm 126

The Lord has done great things for us; we are filled with joy.

D.C.

When the Lord restored the fortunes of · **Zion,**
we were like those who · **dream.**
Then our mouth was filled with · **laughter,**
and our tongue with shouts · **of** joy. R.

Then it was said among the · **nations,**
"The Lord has done great things for · **them."**
The Lord has done great things for · **us,**
and we · **re**-joiced. R.

Restore our fortunes, O · **Lord,**
like the watercourses in the desert of the · **Negev.**
May those who sow in · **tears**
reap with shouts · **of** joy. R.

Those who go out · **weeping,**
bearing the seed for · **sowing,**
shall come home with shouts of · **joy,**
carrying · **their** sheaves. R.

Thirtieth Sunday in Ordinary Time – B

Psalm 126

Guitar

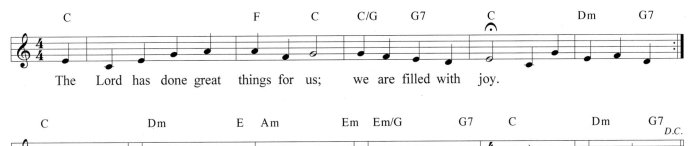

The Lord has done great things for us; we are filled with joy.

When the Lord restored the fortunes of · **Zion,**
we were like those who · **dream.**
Then our mouth was filled with · **laughter,**
and our tongue with shouts · **of** joy. R.

Then it was said among the · **nations,**
"The Lord has done great things for · **them.**"
The Lord has done great things for · **us,**
and we · **re**-joiced. R.

Restore our fortunes, O · **Lord,**
like the watercourses in the desert of the · **Negev.**
May those who sow in · **tears**
reap with shouts · **of** joy. R.

Those who go out · **weeping,**
bearing the seed for · **sowing,**
shall come home with shouts of · **joy,**
carrying · **their** sheaves. R.

C Instrument

B♭ Instrument

Thirty-first Sunday in Ordinary Time – B

Psalm 18

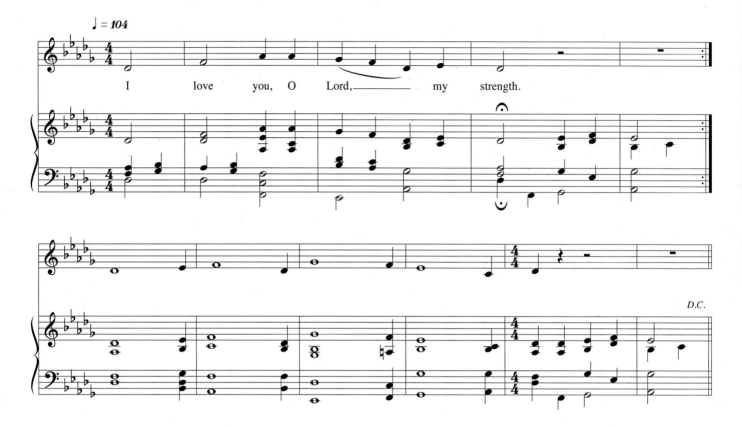

I love you, O Lord, my · **strength.**
The Lord is my rock, my fortress, and my de·-**liverer.**
My God, my rock in whom I take · **refuge,**
my shield, and the source of my salvation, · **my** stronghold. R.

I call upon the Lord, who is worthy to be · **praised,**
so I shall be saved from my · **enemies.**
From his temple he heard my · **voice,**
and my cry to him reached · **his** ears. R.

The Lord lives! Blessed be my · **rock,**
and exalted be the God of my sal·-**vation.**
Great triumphs he gives to his · **king,**
and shows steadfast love to · **his_a**-nointed. R.

Thirty-first Sunday in Ordinary Time – B

Psalm 18

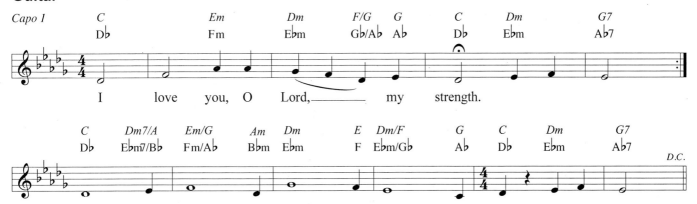

I love you, O Lord, my · **strength.**
The Lord is my rock, my fortress, and my de·-**liverer.**
My God, my rock in whom I take · **refuge,**
my shield, and the source of my salvation, · **my** stronghold. R.

I call upon the Lord, who is worthy to be · **praised,**
so I shall be saved from my · **enemies.**
From his temple he heard my · **voice,**
and my cry to him reached · **his** ears. R.

The Lord lives! Blessed be my · **rock,**
and exalted be the God of my sal·-**vation.**
Great triumphs he gives to his · **king,**
and shows steadfast love to · **his_a**-nointed. R.

Thirty-second Sunday in Ordinary Time – B

Psalm 146

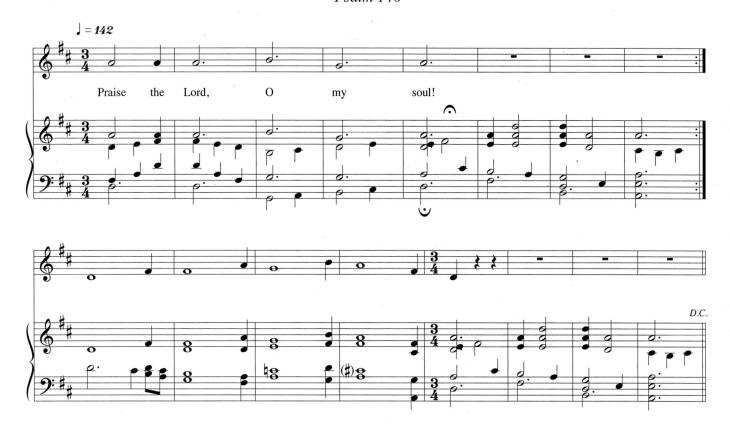

Praise the Lord, O my soul!

It is the Lord who keeps faith for·-**ever,**
who executes justice for the op·-**pressed;**
who gives food to the · **hungry.**
The Lord sets the · **prisoners** free. R.

The Lord opens the eyes of the · **blind**
and lifts up those who are bowed · **down;**
the Lord loves the · **righteous**
and watches over · **the** strangers. R.

The Lord upholds the orphan and the · **widow,**
but the way of the wicked he brings to · **ruin.**
The Lord will reign for·-**ever,**
your God, O Zion, for all · **gener**-ations. R.

224

Thirty-second Sunday in Ordinary Time – B

Psalm 146

Guitar

Praise the Lord, O my soul!

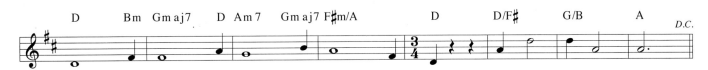

It is the Lord who keeps faith for·-**ever,**
who executes justice for the op·-**pressed;**
who gives food to the · **hungry.**
The Lord sets the · **prisoners** free. R.

The Lord opens the eyes of the · **blind**
and lifts up those who are bowed · **down;**
the Lord loves the · **righteous**
and watches over · **the** strangers. R.

The Lord upholds the orphan and the · **widow,**
but the way of the wicked he brings to · **ruin.**
The Lord will reign for·-**ever,**
your God, O Zion, for all · **gener**-ations. R.

C Instrument

B♭ Instrument

Thirty-third Sunday in Ordinary Time – B

Psalm 16

Pro-tect me, O God,_____ for in you I take re-fuge._____

D.C.

The Lord is my chosen portion · **and_my** cup;
you hold · **my** lot.
I keep the Lord always · **be**-fore_me;
because he is at my right hand, I shall · **not** be moved. R.

Therefore my heart is glad, and my soul · **re**-joices;
my body also rests · **se**-cure.
For you do not give me up · **to** Sheol,
or let your faithful one · **see** the Pit. R.

You show me the path · **of** life.
In your presence there is fullness · **of** joy;
in your right hand · **are** pleasures
for·-**ev**-er-more. R.

Thirty-third Sunday in Ordinary Time – B

Psalm 16

Guitar

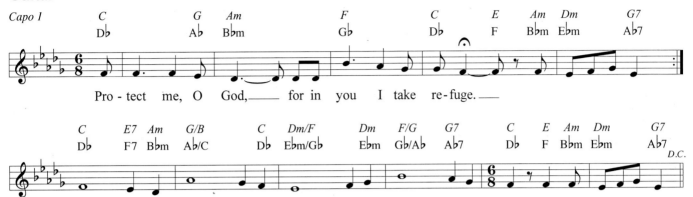

Pro-tect me, O God,___ for in you I take re-fuge. ___

The Lord is my chosen portion · **and_my** cup;
you hold · **my** lot.
I keep the Lord always · **be**-fore_me;
because he is at my right hand, I shall · **not** be moved. R.

Therefore my heart is glad, and my soul · **re**-joices;
my body also rests · **se**-cure.
For you do not give me up · **to** Sheol,
or let your faithful one · **see** the Pit. R.

You show me the path · **of** life.
In your presence there is fullness · **of** joy;
in your right hand · **are** pleasures
for·-**ev**-er-more. R.

C Instrument

B♭ Instrument

Thirty-fourth Sunday in Ordinary Time (Christ the King) – B

Psalm 93

The Lord is king; he is robed in maj-es-ty.

The Lord is king, he is robed · **in** majesty;
the Lord · **is** robed,
he is · **girded** with strength. R.

He has established the world; it shall never · **be** moved;
your throne is established · **from_of** old;
you are from · **ev**-er-lasting. R.

Your decrees are · **very** sure;
holiness befits · **your** house,
O Lord, for·-**ev**-er-more. R.

Thirty-fourth Sunday in Ordinary Time (Christ the King) – B

Psalm 93

Guitar

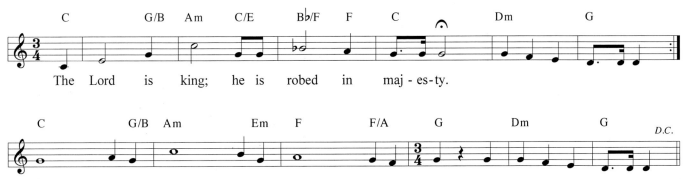

The Lord is king; he is robed in maj-es-ty.

The Lord is king, he is robed · **in** majesty;
the Lord · **is** robed,
he is · **girded** with strength. R.

He has established the world; it shall never · **be** moved;
your throne is established · **from_of** old;
you are from · **ev**-er-lasting. R.

Your decrees are · **very** sure;
holiness befits · **your** house,
O Lord, for·-**ev**-er-more. R.

C Instrument

B♭ Instrument

February 2 – Presentation of the Lord – ABC

Psalm 24

The Lord of hosts, he is king of glory!

Lift up your heads, · **O** gates!
and be lifted up, O · **ancient** doors!
that the King of glory · **may_come** in. R.

Who is the King · **of** glory?
The Lord, strong · **and** mighty,
the Lord, mighty · **in** battle. R.

Lift up your heads, · **O** gates!
and be lifted up, O · **ancient** doors!
that the King of glory · **may_come** in. R.

Who is this King · **of** glory?
The Lord · **of** hosts,
he is the King · **of** glory. R.

February 2 – Presentation of the Lord – ABC

Psalm 24

Guitar

The Lord of hosts, he is king of glo - ry!

Lift up your heads, · **O** gates!
and be lifted up, O · **ancient** doors!
that the King of glory · **may_come** in. R.

Who is the King · **of** glory?
The Lord, strong · **and** mighty,
the Lord, mighty · **in** battle. R.

Lift up your heads, · **O** gates!
and be lifted up, O · **ancient** doors!
that the King of glory · **may_come** in. R.

Who is this King · **of** glory?
The Lord · **of** hosts,
he is the King · **of** glory. R.

C Instrument

B♭ Instrument

March 19 – St. Joseph, Husband of the Blessed Virgin Mary – ABC

Psalm 89

His line shall con - tin - ue for - ev - er.

I will sing of your steadfast love, O Lord, for·-**ever;**
with my mouth I will proclaim your faithfulness to all gener·-**ations.**
I declare that your steadfast love is established for·-**ever;**
your faithfulness is as firm · **as_the** heavens. R.

You said, "I have made a covenant with my · **chosen_one,**
I have sworn to my servant · **David:**
I will establish your descendants for·-**ever,**
and build your throne for all · **gener**-ations." R.

He shall cry to me, "You are my · **Father,**
my God, and the Rock of my sal·-**vation!**"
Forever I will keep my steadfast · **love_for_him,**
and my covenant with him will · **stand** firm. R.

March 19 – St. Joseph, Husband of the Blessed Virgin Mary – ABC

Psalm 89

Guitar

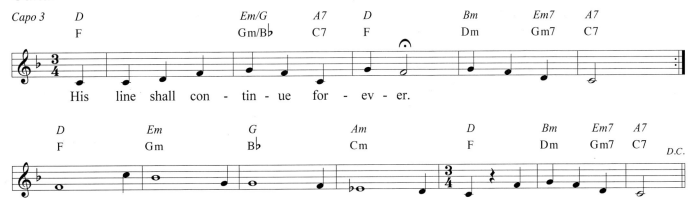

His line shall con - tin - ue for - ev - er.

I will sing of your steadfast love, O Lord, for·-**ever**;
with my mouth I will proclaim your faithfulness to all gener·-**ations.**
I declare that your steadfast love is established for·-**ever**;
your faithfulness is as firm · **as_the** heavens. R.

You said, "I have made a covenant with my · **chosen_one,**
I have sworn to my servant · **David:**
I will establish your descendants for·-**ever,**
and build your throne for all · **gener**-ations." R.

He shall cry to me, "You are my · **Father,**
my God, and the Rock of my sal·-**vation!**"
Forever I will keep my steadfast · **love_for_him,**
and my covenant with him will · **stand** firm. R.

C Instrument

B♭ Instrument

March 25 – Annunciation of the Lord – ABC

Psalm 40

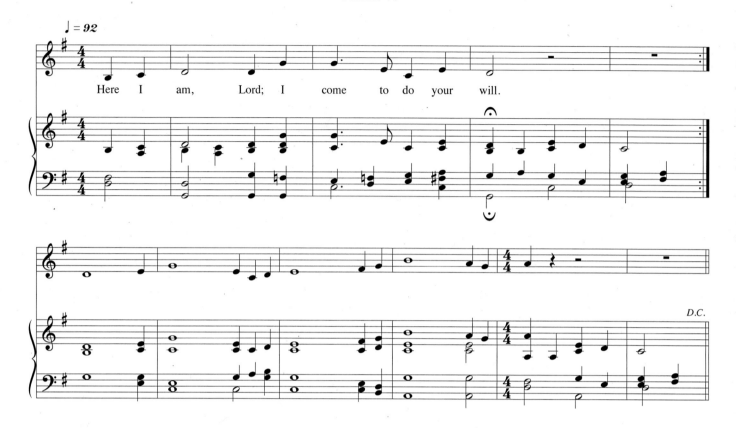

Here I am, Lord; I come to do your will.

Sacrifice and offering you do not de·-**sire,**
but you have given me an · **o**-pen ear.
Burnt offering · **and** sin_offering
you have · **not** re-quired. R.

Then I said, "Here I · **am;**
in the scroll of the book it is · **written** of me.
I delight to do your will, O · **my** God;
your law is with·-**in** my heart." R.

I have told the glad news of de·-**liverance**
in the great · **con**-gre-gation;
see, I have not restrained · **my** lips,
as you · **know,** O Lord. R.

I have not hidden your saving help within my · **heart,**
I have spoken of your faithfulness and · **your** sal-vation;
I have not concealed your steadfast love and · **your** faithfulness
from the great · **con**-gre-gation. R.

March 25 – Annunciation of the Lord – ABC

Psalm 40

Guitar

Here I am, Lord; I come to do your will.

Sacrifice and offering you do not de·-**sire,**
but you have given me an · **o**-pen ear.
Burnt offering · **and** sin_offering
you have · **not** re-quired. R.

Then I said, "Here I · **am;**
in the scroll of the book it is · **written** of me.
I delight to do your will, O · **my** God;
your law is with·-**in** my heart." R.

I have told the glad news of de·-**liverance**
in the great · **con**-gre-gation;
see, I have not restrained · **my** lips,
as you · **know,** O Lord. R.

I have not hidden your saving help within my · **heart,**
I have spoken of your faithfulness and · **your** sal-vation;
I have not concealed your steadfast love and · **your** faithfulness
from the great · **con**-gre-gation. R.

C Instrument

B♭ Instrument

June 24 – Nativity of St. John the Baptist (Vigil) – ABC

Psalm 71

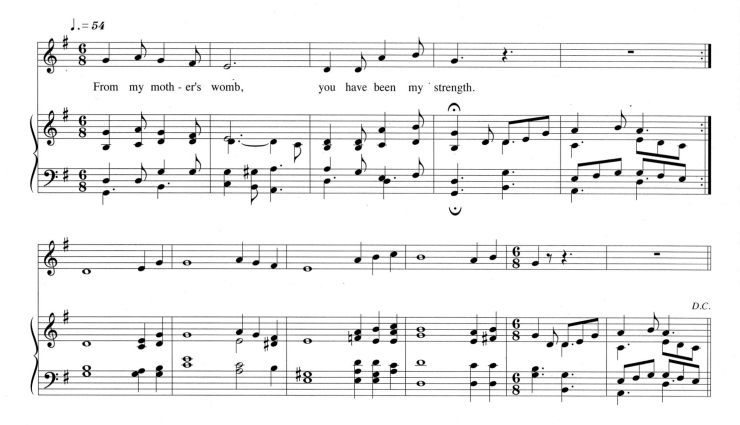

From my moth-er's womb, you have been my strength.

In you, O Lord, I · **take** refuge;
let me never be · **put** to shame.
In your righteousness de··**liver_me** and rescue_me;
incline your ear to · **me** and save_me. R.

Be to me a rock · **of** refuge,
a strong · **fortress,** to save_me,
for you are my rock · **and** my fortress.
Rescue me, O my God, from the · **hand_of** the wicked. R.

For you, O Lord, are · **my** hope,
my trust, O Lord, · **from** my youth.
Upon you I have leaned · **from** my birth;
from my mother's womb you have · **been** my strength. R.

My mouth will tell of your right··**eous** acts,
of your deeds of salvation · **all** day long.
O God, from my youth · **you** have taught_me,
and I still proclaim your · **won**-drous deeds. R.

June 24 – Nativity of St. John the Baptist (Vigil) – ABC

Psalm 71

Guitar

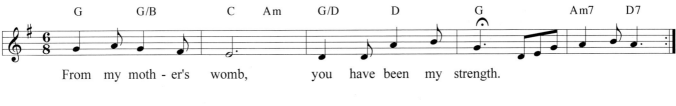

From my moth-er's womb, you have been my strength.

In you, O Lord, I · **take** refuge;
let me never be · **put** to shame.
In your righteousness de·-**liver_me** and rescue_me;
incline your ear to · **me** and save_me. R.

Be to me a rock · **of** refuge,
a strong · **fortress,** to save_me,
for you are my rock · **and** my fortress.
Rescue me, O my God, from the · **hand_of** the wicked. R.

For you, O Lord, are · **my** hope,
my trust, O Lord, · **from** my youth.
Upon you I have leaned · **from** my birth;
from my mother's womb you have · **been** my strength. R.

My mouth will tell of your right·-**eous** acts,
of your deeds of salvation · **all** day long.
O God, from my youth · **you** have taught_me,
and I still proclaim your · **won**-drous deeds. R.

C Instrument

B♭ Instrument

June 24 – Nativity of St. John the Baptist (Day) – ABC

Psalm 139

O Lord, you have searched me and · **known_me.**
You know when I sit down and when I · **rise** up;
you discern my thoughts from far a·-**way.**
You search out my path and my lying down, and are acquainted with all · **my** ways. R.

For it was you who formed my inward · **parts;**
you knit me together in my · **mother's** womb.
I · **praise_you,**
for I am fearfully and · **wonderfully** made. R.

Wonderful are your works; that I know very · **well.**
My frame was not hidden · **from** you,
when I was being made in · **secret,**
intricately woven in the depths of · **the** earth. R.

June 24 – Nativity of St. John the Baptist (Day) – ABC

Psalm 139

Guitar

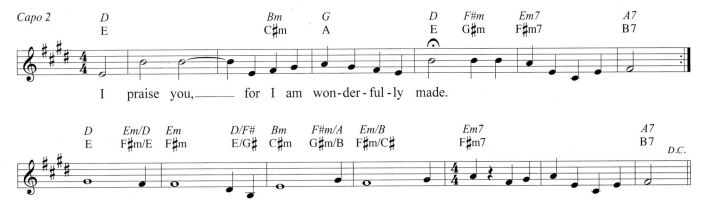

I praise you,——— for I am won-der-ful-ly made.

O Lord, you have searched me and · **known_me.**
You know when I sit down and when I · **rise** up;
you discern my thoughts from far a·-**way.**
You search out my path and my lying down, and are acquainted with all · **my** ways. R.

For it was you who formed my inward · **parts;**
you knit me together in my · **mother's** womb.
I · **praise_you,**
for I am fearfully and · **wonderfully** made. R.

Wonderful are your works; that I know very · **well.**
My frame was not hidden · **from** you,
when I was being made in · **secret,**
intricately woven in the depths of · **the** earth. R.

C Instrument

B♭ Instrument

June 29 – Sts. Peter and Paul, Apostles (Vigil) – ABC

Psalm 19

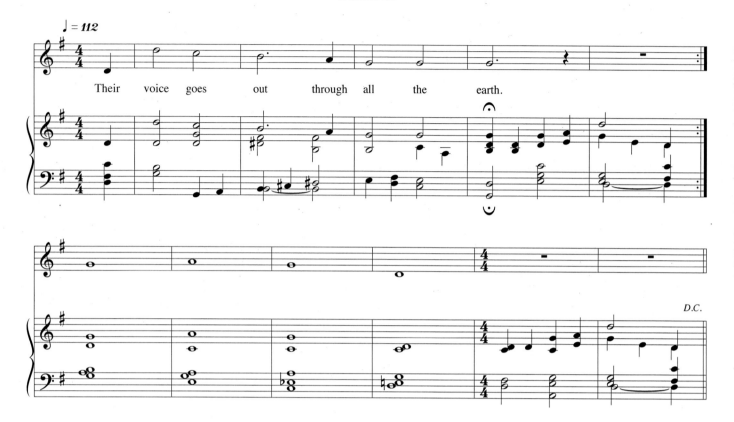

Their voice goes out through all the earth.

The heavens are telling the glory of God;
and the firmament proclaims his handiwork.
Day to day pours forth speech,
and night to night declares knowledge. R.

There is no speech, nor are there words;
their voice is not heard;
yet their voice goes out through all the earth,
and their words to the end of the world. R.

June 29 – Sts. Peter and Paul, Apostles (Vigil) – ABC

Psalm 19

Guitar

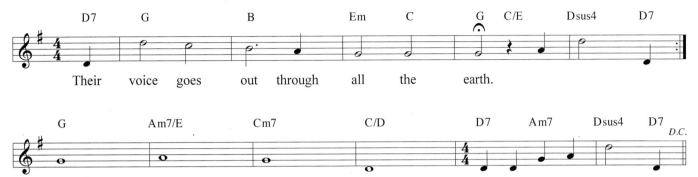

Their voice goes out through all the earth.

The heavens are telling the glory of God;
and the firmament proclaims his handiwork.
Day to day pours forth speech,
and night to night declares knowledge. R.

There is no speech, nor are there words;
their voice is not heard;
yet their voice goes out through all the earth,
and their words to the end of the world. R.

C Instrument

B♭ Instrument

June 29 – Sts. Peter and Paul, Apostles (Day) – ABC

Psalm 34

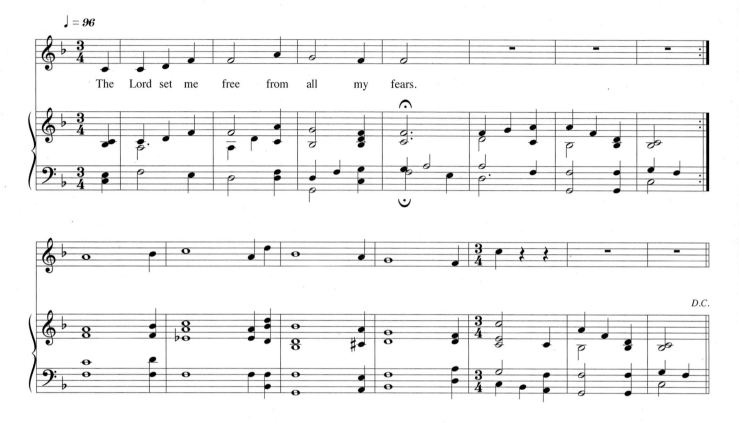

The Lord set me free from all my fears.

I will bless the Lord at all · **times;**
his praise shall continually be in · **my** mouth.
My soul makes its boast in the · **Lord;**
let the humble hear and · **be** glad. R.

O magnify the Lord with · **me,**
and let us exalt his name · **to**-gether.
I sought the Lord, and he · **answered_me,**
and delivered me from all · **my** fears. R.

Look to him, and be · **radiant;**
so your faces shall never · **be_a**-shamed.
The poor one called, and the Lord · **heard,**
and saved that person from ev·-**ery** trouble. R.

The Angel of the Lord en·-**camps**
around those who fear him, and · **de**-livers_them.
O taste and see that the Lord is · **good;**
blessed is the one who takes refuge · **in** him. R.

June 29 – Sts. Peter and Paul, Apostles (Day) – ABC

Psalm 34

Guitar

The Lord set me free from all my fears.

I will bless the Lord at all · **times;**
his praise shall continually be in · **my** mouth.
My soul makes its boast in the · **Lord;**
let the humble hear and · **be** glad. R.

O magnify the Lord with · **me,**
and let us exalt his name · **to**-gether.
I sought the Lord, and he · **answered_me,**
and delivered me from all · **my** fears. R.

Look to him, and be · **radiant;**
so your faces shall never · **be_a**-shamed.
The poor one called, and the Lord · **heard,**
and saved that person from ev·-**ery** trouble. R.

The Angel of the Lord en·-**camps**
around those who fear him, and · **de**-livers_them.
O taste and see that the Lord is · **good;**
blessed is the one who takes refuge · **in** him. R.

C Instrument

B♭ Instrument

August 6 – Transfiguration of the Lord – ABC

Psalm 97

The Lord is king, the most high o-ver all the earth.

The Lord is king! Let the earth re··-**joice;**
let the many coastlands · **be** glad!
Clouds and thick darkness are · **all** around him;
righteousness and justice are the foundation · **of** his throne. R.

The mountains melt like wax before the · **Lord,**
before the Lord of · **all_the** earth.
The heavens pro··-**claim** his righteousness;
and all the peoples be··-**hold** his glory. R.

1 - For you, O Lord, are most high over all the · **earth;**
4 - you are exalted far a··-**bove** all gods. R.

244

August 6 – Transfiguration of the Lord – ABC

Psalm 97

Guitar

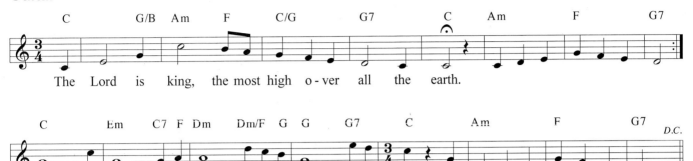

The Lord is king, the most high o-ver all the earth.

The Lord is king! Let the earth re·-**joice;**
let the many coastlands · **be** glad!
Clouds and thick darkness are · **all** around him;
righteousness and justice are the foundation · **of** his throne. R.

The mountains melt like wax before the · **Lord,**
before the Lord of · **all_the** earth.
The heavens pro·-**claim** his righteousness;
and all the peoples be·-**hold** his glory. R.

1 - For you, O Lord, are most high over all the · **earth;**
4 - you are exalted far a·-**bove** all gods. R.

C Instrument

B♭ Instrument

August 15 – Assumption of the Blessed Virgin Mary (Vigil) – ABC

Psalm 132

Rise up, O Lord, and go to your rest-ing place, you____ and the ark of your might.

We heard of the ark in · **Ephrathah;**
we found it in the fields · **of** Jaar.
"Let us go to his · **dwelling_place;**
let us worship · **at_his** footstool." R.

Let your priests be clothed with · **righteousness,**
and let your faithful shout · **for** joy.
For your servant David's · **sake**
do not turn away the face of · **your_a**-nointed_one. R.

For the Lord has chosen · **Zion;**
he has desired it for his ha·-**bi**·-tation.
"This is my resting place for·-**ever;**
here I will reside, for I have · **de**-sired_it." R.

August 15 – Assumption of the Blessed Virgin Mary (Vigil) – ABC

Psalm 132

Guitar

Rise up, O Lord, and go to your rest-ing place, you ___ and the ark of your might.

We heard of the ark in · **Ephrathah;**
we found it in the fields · **of** Jaar.
"Let us go to his · **dwelling_place;**
let us worship · **at_his** footstool." R.

Let your priests be clothed with · **righteousness,**
and let your faithful shout · **for** joy.
For your servant David's · **sake**
do not turn away the face of · **your_a**-nointed_one. R.

For the Lord has chosen · **Zion;**
he has desired it for his ha·-**bi**-tation.
"This is my resting place for·-**ever;**
here I will reside, for I have · **de**-sired_it." R.

C Instrument

B♭ Instrument

August 15 – Assumption of the Blessed Virgin Mary (Day) – ABC

Psalm 45

At your right hand___ stands the queen in gold of O - phir.

Daughters of kings are among your ladies of · **honour;**
at your right hand stands the queen in gold · **of** Ophir.
Hear, O daughter, consider and incline · **your** ear;
forget your people and your · **father's** house. R.

The king will desire your · **beauty.**
Since he is your lord, · **bow** to_him;
The princess is decked with golden robes; in many-coloured robes she is led to · **the** king;
behind her the virgins, her com·-**panions**, follow. R.

1 - With joy and gladness they are led a·-**long**
4 - as they enter the palace · **of_the** king. R.

August 15 – Assumption of the Blessed Virgin Mary (Day) – ABC

Psalm 45

Guitar

At your right hand___ stands the queen in gold of O-phir.

Daughters of kings are among your ladies of · **honour;**
at your right hand stands the queen in gold · **of** Ophir.
Hear, O daughter, consider and incline · **your** ear;
forget your people and your · **father's** house. R.

The king will desire your · **beauty.**
Since he is your · **lord,** bow_to_him;
The princess is decked with golden robes; in many-coloured robes she is led to · **the** king;
behind her the virgins, her com·-**panions,** follow. R.

1 - With joy and gladness they are led a·-**long**
4 - as they enter the palace · **of_the** king. R.

C Instrument

B♭ Instrument

September 14 – Exaltation of the Holy Cross – ABC

Psalm 78

Do not for - get the works of the Lord!

D.C.

Give ear, O my people, to my · **teaching;**
incline your ears to the words of my · **mouth.**
I will open my mouth in a · **parable;**
I will utter dark sayings · **from_of** old. R.

When God killed them, the people · **sought_for_him;**
they repented and sought him · **earnestly.**
They remembered that God was their · **rock,**
the Most High God · **their_re**-deemer. R.

But they flattered him with their · **mouths;**
they lied to him with their · **tongues.**
Their heart was not steadfast toward · **him;**
they were not true to · **his** covenant. R.

Yet he, being compassionate, forgave their in·-**iquity,**
and did not de·-**stroy_them;**
often he restrained his · **anger,**
and did not stir up all · **his** wrath. R.

September 14 – Exaltation of the Holy Cross – ABC

Psalm 78

Guitar

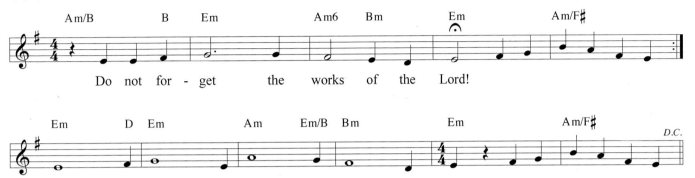

Do not for - get the works of the Lord!

Give ear, O my people, to my · **teaching;**
incline your ears to the words of my · **mouth.**
I will open my mouth in a · **parable;**
I will utter dark sayings · **from_of** old. R.

When God killed them, the people · **sought_for_him;**
they repented and sought him · **earnestly.**
They remembered that God was their · **rock,**
the Most High God · **their_re**-deemer. R.

But they flattered him with their · **mouths;**
they lied to him with their · **tongues.**
Their heart was not steadfast toward · **him;**
they were not true to · **his** covenant. R.

Yet he, being compassionate, forgave their in·-**iquity,**
and did not de·-**stroy_them;**
often he restrained his · **anger,**
and did not stir up all · **his** wrath. R.

C Instrument

B♭ Instrument

November 1 – All Saints – ABC

Psalm 24

Lord, this is the com-pa-ny —— of those who seek your face.

The earth is the Lord's and all that · **is** in_it,
the world, and those · **who** live_in_it;
for he has founded it · **on_the** seas,
and established it · **on_the** river. R.

Who shall ascend the hill · **of_the** Lord?
And who shall stand in his · **holy** place?
Someone who has clean hands and a · **pure** heart,
who does not lift up their soul to · **what_is** false. R.

That person will receive blessing · **from_the** Lord,
and vindication from the God of their · **sal**-vation.
Such is the company of those · **who** seek_him,
who seek the face of the God · **of** Jacob. R.

252

November 1 – All Saints – ABC

Psalm 24

Guitar

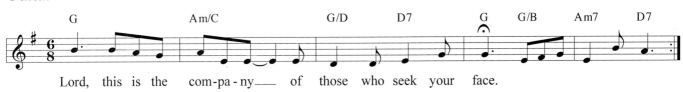

Lord, this is the com-pa-ny___ of those who seek your face.

The earth is the Lord's and all that · **is** in_it,
the world, and those · **who** live_in_it;
for he has founded it · **on_the** seas,
and established it · **on_the** river. R.

Who shall ascend the hill · **of_the** Lord?
And who shall stand in his · **holy** place?
Someone who has clean hands and a · **pure** heart,
who does not lift up their soul to · **what_is** false. R.

That person will receive blessing · **from_the** Lord,
and vindication from the God of their · **sal**-vation.
Such is the company of those · **who** seek_him,
who seek the face of the God · **of** Jacob. R.

C Instrument

B♭ Instrument

November 2 – Commemoration of All the Faithful Departed I – ABC
(All Souls)
Psalm 103

The Lord is merciful and · **gracious,**
slow to anger and abounding in stead·-**fast** love.
He does not deal with us according to our · **sins,**
nor repay us according to our · **in**-iquities. R.

As a father has compassion for his · **children,**
so the Lord has compassion for those · **who** fear_him.
For he knows how we were · **made;**
he remembers that we · **are** dust. R.

As for mortals, their days are like · **grass;**
they flourish like a flower · **of_the** field;
for the wind passes over it, and it is · **gone,**
and its place knows it · **no** more. R.

The steadfast love of the · **Lord**
is from everlasting to everlasting on those · **who** fear_him,
and his righteousness to children's · **children,**
to those who keep his covenant and remember to do his · **com**-mandments. R.

November 2 – Commemoration of All the Faithful Departed I – ABC

(All Souls)

Psalm 103

Guitar

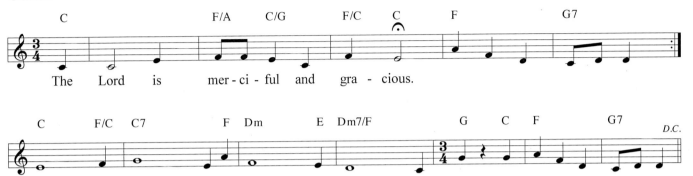

The Lord is mer - ci - ful and gra - cious.

The Lord is merciful and · **gracious,**
slow to anger and abounding in stead·-**fast** love.
He does not deal with us according to our · **sins,**
nor repay us according to our · **in**-iquities. R.

As a father has compassion for his · **children,**
so the Lord has compassion for those · **who** fear_him.
For he knows how we were · **made;**
he remembers that we · **are** dust. R.

As for mortals, their days are like · **grass;**
they flourish like a flower · **of_the** field;
for the wind passes over it, and it is · **gone,**
and its place knows it · **no** more. R.

The steadfast love of the · **Lord**
is from everlasting to everlasting on those · **who** fear_him,
and his righteousness to children's · **children,**
to those who keep his covenant and remember to do his · **com**-mandments. R.

C Instrument

B♭ Instrument

November 2 – Commemoration of All the Faithful Departed II –ABC

(All Souls)

Psalm 23

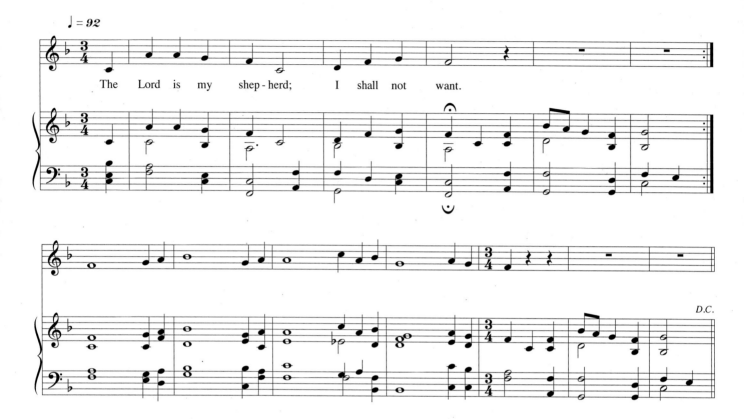

The Lord is my shepherd, I shall · **not** want.
He makes me lie down in · **green** pastures;
he leads me be·-**side** still waters;
he re·-**stores** my soul. R.

He leads me in right paths for his · **name's** sake.
Even though I walk through the darkest valley, I fear · **no** evil;
for · **you** are with_me;
your rod and your · **staff**—they comfort_me. R.

You prepare a table · **be**-fore_me
in the presence · **of_my** enemies;
you anoint my · **head** with oil;
my · **cup** over-flows. R.

Surely goodness and mercy · **shall** follow_me
all the days of · **my** life,
and I shall dwell in the · **house_of** the Lord
my · **whole** life long. R.

November 2 – Commemoration of All the Faithful Departed II –ABC

(All Souls)

Psalm 23

Guitar

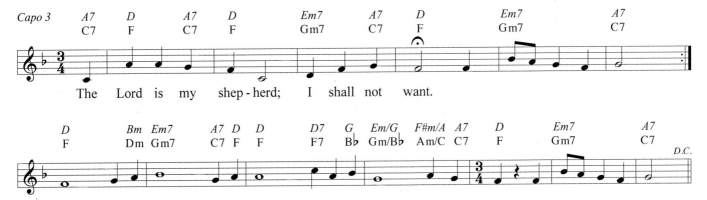

The Lord is my shep-herd; I shall not want.

The Lord is my shepherd, I shall · **not** want.
He makes me lie down in · **green** pastures;
he leads me be·-**side** still waters;
he re·-**stores** my soul. R.

He leads me in right paths for his · **name's** sake.
Even though I walk through the darkest valley, I fear · **no** evil;
for · **you** are with_me;
your rod and your · **staff**—they comfort_me. R.

You prepare a table · **be**-fore_me
in the presence · **of_my** enemies;
you anoint my · **head** with oil;
my · **cup** over-flows. R.

Surely goodness and mercy · **shall** follow_me
all the days of · **my** life,
and I shall dwell in the · **house_of** the Lord
my · **whole** life long. R.

C Instrument

B♭ Instrument

November 2 – Commemoration of All the Faithful Departed III – ABC

(All Souls)

Psalm 116

I will walk be-fore the Lord, in the land of the liv-ing.

Gracious is the Lord, and · **righteous;**
our God · **is** merciful.
The Lord protects the · **simple;**
when I was brought low, · **he** saved_me. R.

I kept my faith, even when I · **said,**
"I am greatly · **af**-flicted";
I said in my conster-·**nation,**
"Everyone is · **a** liar." R.

Precious in the sight of the · **Lord**
is the death of · **his** faithful_ones.
O Lord, I am your · **servant;**
you have loosed · **my** bonds. R.

November 2 – Commemoration of All the Faithful Departed III – ABC

(All Souls)

Psalm 116

Guitar

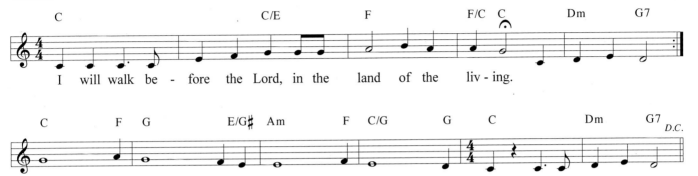

I will walk be - fore the Lord, in the land of the liv - ing.

Gracious is the Lord, and · **righteous;**
our God · **is** merciful.
The Lord protects the · **simple;**
when I was brought low, · **he** saved_me. R.

I kept my faith, even when I · **said,**
"I am greatly · **af**-flicted";
I said in my conster·-**nation,**
"Everyone is · **a** liar." R.

Precious in the sight of the · **Lord**
is the death of · **his** faithful_ones.
O Lord, I am your · **servant;**
you have loosed · **my** bonds. R.

C Instrument

B♭ Instrument

November 9 – Dedication of the Lateran Basilica – ABC

Psalm 46

The streams make glad the cit-y of God, the ha-bi-ta-tion of the Most High.

God is our · **refuge** and strength,
a very present · **help** in trouble.
Therefore we will not fear, though the · **earth** should change,
though the mountains · **shake_in** the heart_of the sea. R.

There is a river whose streams make glad the · **city** of God,
the holy habitation · **of_the** Most High.
God is in the midst of the city; it shall · **not** be moved;
God will · **help_it** when_the morn-ing dawns. R.

The Lord of · **hosts** is with_us;
the God of Jacob · **is** our refuge.
Come, behold the · **works_of** the Lord;
see what awesome · **things_he** has brought_on the earth. R.

November 9 – Dedication of the Lateran Basilica – ABC

Psalm 46

Guitar

The streams make glad the cit-y of God, the ha-bi-ta-tion of the Most High.

God is our · **refuge** and strength,
a very present · **help** in trouble.
Therefore we will not fear, though the · **earth** should change,
though the mountains · **shake_in** the heart_of the sea. R.

There is a river whose streams make glad the · **city** of God,
the holy habitation · **of_the** Most High.
God is in the midst of the city; it shall · **not** be moved;
God will · **help_it** when_the morn-ing dawns. R.

The Lord of · **hosts** is with_us;
the God of Jacob · **is** our refuge.
Come, behold the · **works_of** the Lord;
see what awesome · **things_he** has brought_on the earth. R.

C Instrument

B♭ Instrument

December 8 – Immaculate Conception of the Blessed Virgin Mary – ABC

Psalm 98

O sing to the Lord · **a new song,**
for he has done · **marvel**-lous things.
His right hand and his · **ho**-ly arm
have · **brought** him victory. R.

The Lord has made · **known** his victory;
he has revealed his vindication in the · **sight_of** the nations.
He has remembered his · **stead**-fast love
and faithfulness to the · **house** of Israel. R.

All the ends of the · **earth** have seen
the victory · **of** our God.
Make a joyful noise to the Lord, · **all** the earth;
break forth into joyous · **song_and** sing praises. R.

December 8 – Immaculate Conception of the Blessed Virgin Mary – ABC

Psalm 98

Guitar

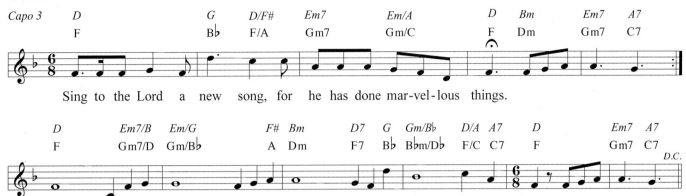

Sing to the Lord a new song, for he has done mar-vel-lous things.

O sing to the Lord · **a** new song,
for he has done · **marvel**-lous things.
His right hand and his · **ho**-ly arm
have · **brought** him victory. R.

The Lord has made · **known** his victory;
he has revealed his vindication in the · **sight_of** the nations.
He has remembered his · **stead**-fast love
and faithfulness to the · **house** of Israel. R.

All the ends of the · **earth** have seen
the victory · **of** our God.
Make a joyful noise to the Lord, · **all** the earth;
break forth into joyous · **song_and** sing praises. R.

C Instrument

B♭ Instrument

Table of Responsorial Psalms and Canticles

085. 8ab-9, 10-11, 12-13	Year B - Second Sunday of Advent
085. 8ab-9, 10-11, 12-13	Year A - Nineteenth Sunday in Ordinary Time
086. 5-6, 9-10, 15-16	Year A - Sixteenth Sunday in Ordinary Time
089. 1-2, 3-4, 26+28	Years ABC - Joseph, Husband of Mary
089. 1-2, 3-4, 26+28	Year B - Fourth Sunday of Advent
089. 1-2, 15-16, 17-18	Year A - Thirteenth Sunday in Ordinary Time
089. 3-4, 15-16, 26+28	Years ABC - Vigil of Christmas
089. 20-21, 24+26, 27-28	Years ABC - Mass of Chrism
090. 1-2, 3-4, 5-6, 14+16	Years ABC - Ext Vigil of Pentecost 6
090. 3-4, 5-6, 12-13, 14+17	Year C - Twenty-third Sunday in Ordinary Time
090. 3-4, 5-6, 12-13, 14+17	Year C - Eighteenth Sunday in Ordinary Time
090. 12-13, 14-15, 16-17	Year B - Twenty-eighth Sunday in Ordinary Time
091. 1-2, 10-11, 12-13, 14-15	Years ABC - Common for Lent
091. 1-2, 10-11, 12-13, 14-15	Year C - First Sunday of Lent
092. 1-2, 12-13, 14-15	Year C - Eighth Sunday in Ordinary Time
092. 1-2, 12-13, 14-15	Year B - Eleventh Sunday in Ordinary Time
093. 1ab, 1c-2, 5	Year B - Christ the King
095. 1-2, 6-7ab, 7c-9	Years ABC - Common for Ordinary Time
095. 1-2, 6-7ab, 7c-9	Year C - Twenty-seventh Sunday in Ordinary Time
095. 1-2, 6-7ab, 7c-9	Year B - Fourth Sunday in Ordinary Time
095. 1-2, 6-7ab, 7c-9	Year A - Twenty-third Sunday in Ordinary Time
095. 1-2, 6-7ab, 7c-9	Year A - Third Sunday of Lent
096. 1-2, 3-4, 11-12, 13	Years ABC - Christmas during the night
096. 1-2, 3-4, 7-8, 9-10ac	Year C - Second Sunday in Ordinary Time
096. 1+3, 4-5, 7-8, 9+10ac	Year A - Twenty-ninth Sunday in Ordinary Time
097. 1-2, 3-4, 5-6, 11-12	Years ABC - Ext Vigil of Pentecost 3
097. 1-2, 5-6, 9+12	Years ABC - Transfiguration of the Lord
097. 1-2, 5-6, 11-12	Years ABC - Christmas at dawn
097. 1-2, 6-7ac, 9+12	Year C - Seventh Sunday of Easter
098. 1, 2-3ab, 3cd-4	Years ABC - Immaculate Conception
098. 1, 2-3ab, 3cd-4	Year C - Twenty-eighth Sunday in Ordinary Time
098. 1, 2-3ab, 3cd-4	Year B - Sixth Sunday of Easter
098. 1, 2-3a, 3b-4, 5-6	Years ABC - Christmas during the day
098. 1, 2-3a, 3b-4, 5-6	Years ABC - Common for Christmas
098. 5-6, 7-8, 9	Year C - Thirty-third Sunday in Ordinary Time
100. 1-2, 3, 4, 5	Year A - Eleventh Sunday in Ordinary Time
100. 1-2, 3, 5	Years ABC - Common for Ordinary Time
100. 1-2, 3, 5	Year C - Fourth Sunday of Easter
103. 1-2, 3-4, 6-7, 8-9	Year A - Sacred Heart of Jesus
103. 1-2, 3-4, 6-7, 8+11	Year C - Third Sunday of Lent
103. 1-2, 3-4, 8+10, 12-13	Years ABC - Common for Ordinary Time
103. 1-2, 3-4, 8+10, 12-13	Year C - Seventh Sunday in Ordinary Time
103. 1-2, 3-4, 8+10, 12-13	Year B - Eighth Sunday in Ordinary Time
103. 1-2, 3-4, 8+10, 12-13	Year A - Seventh Sunday in Ordinary Time
103. 1-2, 3-4, 9-10, 11-12	Year A - Twenty-fourth Sunday in Ordinary Time
103. 1-2, 11-12, 19-20	Year B - Seventh Sunday of Easter
103. 8+10, 13-14, 15-16, 17	Years ABC - All Souls I
104. 1b-2, 3-4, 24-25, 27+28 &c	Year C - Baptism of the Lord
104. 1-2a, 5-6, 10+12, 13-14, &c	Years ABC - Easter Vigil 1.1
104. 1-2a, 24+25c, 27-28, 29&c	Years ABC - Ext Vigil of Pentecost 7
104. 1-2a, 24+25c, 27-28, 29&c	Years ABC - Vigil of Pentecost
104. 1ab+24ac, 29b-30, 31+34	Years ABC - Common for Pentecost
104. 1ab+24ac, 29b-30, 31+34	Year A - Pentecost Sunday
104. 1ab+24ac, 29b-30, 31+34	Year B - Pentecost Sunday
104. 1ab+24ac, 29b-30, 31+34	Year C - Pentecost Sunday
105. 1-2, 3-4, 5-6, 8-9	Year B - Holy Family
105. 1-2, 5-6, 7+8a+9a+10b	Years ABC - Ext Vigil of Pentecost 5
107. 23-24, 25-26, 28-29, 30-31	Year B - Twelfth Sunday in Ordinary Time
110. 1, 2, 3, 4	Year C - Body and Blood of Christ
112. 4-5, 6-7, 8a-9	Year A - Fifth Sunday in Ordinary Time
113. 1-2, 4-6, 7-8	Year C - Twenty-fifth Sunday in Ordinary Time

116. 1-2, 3-4, 5-6, 8-9	Year B - Twenty-fourth Sunday in Ordinary Time
116. 5-6, 10-11, 15-16	Years ABC - All Souls III
116. 10+15, 16-17, 18-19	Year B - Second Sunday of Lent
116. 12-13, 15-16, 17-18	Years ABC - Mass of the Lord's Supper
116. 12-13, 15-16, 17-18	Year B - Body and Blood of Christ
117. 1, 2	Year C - Twenty-first Sunday in Ordinary Time
117. 1, 2	Year C - Ninth Sunday in Ordinary Time
118. 1-2, 16-17, 22-23	Years ABC - Common for Easter
118. 1-2, 16-17, 22-23	Years ABC - Easter Sunday
118. 1-2, 16-17, 22-23	Years ABC - Easter Vigil - Solemn Alleluia
118. 1+8-9, 21-23, 26+28-29	Year B - Fourth Sunday of Easter
118. 2-4, 13-15, 22-24	Year A - Second Sunday of Easter
118. 2-4, 16-18, 22-24	Year B - Second Sunday of Easter
118. 2-4, 22-24, 25-27a	Year C - Second Sunday of Easter
119. 1-2, 4-5, 17-18, 33-34	Year A - Sixth Sunday in Ordinary Time
119. 57+72, 76-77, 127-128, &c	Year A - Seventeenth Sunday in Ordinary Time
121. 1-2, 3-4, 5-6, 7-8	Year C - Twenty-ninth Sunday in Ordinary Time
122. 1-2, 3-4a, 4b-5	Year C - Christ the King
122. 1-2, 3-4a, 4b-5, 6-7, 8-9	Years ABC - Common Last Weeks of Ordinary Time
122. 1-2, 4-5, 6-7, 8-9	Year A - First Sunday of Advent
123. 1-2a, 2b, 3-4	Year B - Fourteenth Sunday in Ordinary Time
126. 1-2a, 2b-3, 4-5, 6	Year C - Fifth Sunday of Lent
126. 1-2a, 2b-3, 4-5, 6	Year C - Second Sunday of Advent
126. 1-2a, 2b-3, 4-5, 6	Year B - Thirtieth Sunday in Ordinary Time
128. 1-2, 3, 4-5	Year B - Twenty-seventh Sunday in Ordinary Time
128. 1-2, 3, 4-5	Year A - Thirty-third Sunday in Ordinary Time
128. 1-2, 3, 4-5	Years ABC - Holy Family
130. 1-2, 3-4, 5-6, 7b-8	Years ABC - Common for Lent
130. 1-2, 3-4, 5-6, 7b-8	Year B - Tenth Sunday in Ordinary Time
130. 1-2, 3-4, 5-6, 7b-8	Year A - Fifth Sunday of Lent
131. 1, 2, 3	Year A - Thirty-first Sunday in Ordinary Time
132. 6-7, 9-10, 13-14	Years ABC - Vigil of the Assumption
137. 1-2, 3-4, 5-6	Year B - Fourth Sunday of Lent
138. 1-2a, 2b-3, 4-5, 7c-8	Year C - Fifth Sunday in Ordinary Time
138. 1-2a, 2b-3, 6-7ab, 7c-8	Year C - Seventeenth Sunday in Ordinary Time
138. 1-2a, 2b-3, 6+8b	Year A - Twenty-first Sunday in Ordinary Time
139. 1-3, 4+6, 7-8, 10+17	Years ABC - Ext Vigil of Pentecost 4
139. 1-3, 13-14a, 14b-15	Years ABC - Birth of John the Baptist
145. 1-2, 8-9, 10-11, 13cd-14	Years ABC - Common for Ordinary Time
145. 1-2, 8-9, 10-11, 13cd-14	Year C - Thirty-first Sunday in Ordinary Time
145. 1-2, 8-9, 10-11, 13cd-14	Year A - Fourteenth Sunday in Ordinary Time
145. 2-3, 8-9, 17-18	Year A - Twenty-fifth Sunday in Ordinary Time
145. 8-9, 10-11, 12-13	Year C - Fifth Sunday of Easter
145. 8-9, 15-16, 17-18	Year A - Eighteenth Sunday in Ordinary Time
145. 10-11, 15-16, 17-18	Year B - Seventeenth Sunday in Ordinary Time
146. 6c-7, 8-9a, 9b-10	Years ABC - Common for Advent
146. 6c-7, 8-9a, 9b-10	Year C - Twenty-sixth Sunday in Ordinary Time
146. 6c-7, 8-9a, 9b-10	Year B - Thirty-second Sunday in Ordinary Time
146. 6c-7, 8-9a, 9b-10	Year B - Twenty-third Sunday in Ordinary Time
146. 6c-7, 8-9a, 9b-10	Year A - Fourth Sunday in Ordinary Time
146. 6c-7, 8-9a, 9b-10	Year A - Third Sunday of Advent
147. 1-2, 3-4, 5-6	Year B - Fifth Sunday in Ordinary Time
147. 12-13, 14-15, 19-20	Years ABC - Second Sunday after Christmas
147. 12-13, 14-15, 19-20	Year A - Body and Blood of Christ
Daniel 3. 52, 53, 54, 55, 56	Year A - Trinity Sunday
Exodus 15.1-2, 3-5, 6-7, 17-18	Years ABC - Easter Vigil 3
Isaiah 12. 2-3, 4bcd, 5-6	Years ABC - Easter Vigil 5
Isaiah 12. 2-3, 4bcd, 5-6	Year B - Sacred Heart of Jesus
Isaiah 12. 2-3, 4bcd, 5-6	Year B - Baptism of the Lord
Isaiah 12. 3, 4bcd, 5-6	Year C - Third Sunday of Advent
Luke 1. 47-48, 49-50, 53-54	Year B - Third Sunday of Advent

267

Table of Psalm Refrains

Refrain	Psalm	
A light will shine on us this day: The Lord is born for us.	097. 1-2, 5-6, 11-12	Years ABC - Christmas at dawn
All the ends of the earth have seen the victory of our God.	098. 1, 2-3a, 3b-4, 5-6	Years ABC - Christmas during the day
	098. 1, 2-3a, 3b-4, 5-6	Years ABC - Common for Christmas
Alleluia! Alleluia! Alleluia!	118. 1-2, 16-17, 22-23	Years ABC - Easter Vigil - Alleluia
As a deer longs for flowing streams, my soul longs for you, O God.	042. 2, 4bcd; 43.3, 4,	Years ABC - Easter Vigil 7.1
Ascribe to the Lord glory and strength.	096. 1+3, 4-5, 7-8, 9+10ac	Year A - Twenty-ninth Sunday in OT
At your right hand stands the queen in gold of Ophir.	045. 9-10, 11+12c+14, 15-17	Years ABC - Assumption
Be with me, Lord, when I am in trouble.	091. 1-2, 10-11, 12-13, 14-15	Year C - First Sunday of Lent
	091. 1-2, 10-11, 12-13, 14-15	Years ABC - Common for Lent
Before the Angels I sing your praise, O Lord.	138. 1-2a, 2b-3, 4-5, 7c-8	Year C - Fifth Sunday in OT
Blessed are the poor in spirit; the kingdom of heaven is theirs!	146. 6c-7, 8-9a, 9b-10	Year A - Fourth Sunday in OT
Blessed are those who live in your house, O Lord.	084. 1-2, 4-5, 8-9, 10	Year C - Holy Family
Blessed are those who walk in the law of the Lord!	119. 1-2, 4-5, 17-18, 33-34	Year A - Sixth Sunday in OT
Blessed is everyone who fears the Lord.	128. 1-2, 3, 4-5	Year A - Thirty-third Sunday in OT
Blessed is everyone who fears the Lord, who walks in his ways.	128. 1-2, 3, 4-5	Years ABC - Holy Family
Blessed the one who fears the Lord.	034. 1-2, 9-10, 11-12, 13-14	Years ABC - Common for Christmas
Blessed the one who trusts in the Lord.	001. 1-2, 3, 4+6	Year C - Sixth Sunday in OT
Blessed the people the Lord has chosen as his heritage.	033. 1+12, 18-19, 20+22	Year C - Nineteenth Sunday in OT
	033. 4-5, 6+9, 18-19, 20+22	Year B - Trinity Sunday
Create in me a clean heart, O God.	051. 1-2, 10-11, 12-13	Year B - Fifth Sunday of Lent
	051. 10-11, 12-13, 16-17	Years ABC - Easter Vigil 7.2
Declare the marvellous works of the Lord among all the peoples.	096. 1-2, 3-4, 7-8, 9-10ac	Year C - Second Sunday in OT
Do not forget the works of the Lord!	078. 1-2, 34-35, 36-37, 38	Years ABC - Exaltation of the Holy Cross
Father, into your hands I commend my spirit.	031. 1+5, 11-12, 14-15, 16+24	Years ABC - The Lord's Passion
Fill us with your love, O Lord, that we may rejoice and be glad.	090. 12-13, 14-15, 16-17	Year B - Twenty-eighth Sunday in OT
Forever I will sing of your steadfast love, O Lord.	089. 1-2, 3-4, 26+28	Year B - Fourth Sunday of Advent
	089. 1-2, 15-16, 17-18	Year A - Thirteenth Sunday in OT
	089. 3-4, 15-16, 26+28	Years ABC - Vigil of Christmas
	089. 20-21, 24+26, 27-28	Years ABC - Mass of Chrism
For God alone my soul waits in silence.	062. 1-2, 5-6, 7-8	Year A - Eighth Sunday in OT
From my mother's womb, you have been my strength.	071. 1-2, 3, 5-6, 15+17	Years ABC - John the Baptist (Vigil)
Give thanks to the Lord for he is good; his steadfast love endures forever.	118. 2-4, 13-15, 22-24	Year A - Second Sunday of Easter
	118. 2-4, 16-18, 22-24	Year B - Second Sunday of Easter
	118. 2-4, 22-24, 25-27a	Year C - Second Sunday of Easter
Give thanks to the Lord; his steadfast love endures forever.	107. 23-24, 25-26, 28-29, 30-31	Year B - Twelfth Sunday in OT
Give us your spirit, O Lord, and we shall live.	090. 1-2, 3-4, 5-6, 14+16	Years ABC - Ext Vigil of Pentecost 6
Glory and praise for ever!	Daniel 3. 52, 53, 54, 55, 56	Year A - Trinity Sunday

Response	Reference	Occasion
Go into all the world and proclaim the good news.	117. 1, 2	Year C - Ninth Sunday in OT
	117. 1, 2	Year C - Twenty-first Sunday in OT
God has gone up with a shout, the Lord with the sound of a trumpet.	047. 1-2, 5-6, 7-8	Year A - Ascension of the Lord
	047. 1-2, 5-6, 7-8	Year B - Ascension of the Lord
	047. 1-2, 5-6, 7-8	Year C - Ascension of the Lord
	047. 1-2, 5-6, 7-8	Years ABC - Common for Ascension
Have mercy, O Lord, for we have sinned.	051. 1-2, 3-4a, 10-11, 12+15	Year A - First Sunday of Lent
	051. 1-2, 3-4a, 10-11, 12+15	Years ABC - Ash Wednesday
	051. 1-2, 3-4a, 10-11, 12+15	Years ABC - Common for Lent
Heal me, O Lord, for I have sinned against you.	041. 1-2, 3-4, 12-13	Year B - Seventh Sunday in OT
Here I am, Lord; I come to do your will.	040. 1+3a, 6, 7-8, 9	Year A - Second Sunday in OT
	040. 1+3a, 6, 7-8, 9	Year B - Second Sunday in OT
	040. 6, 7-8, 9, 10	Years ABC - Annunciation of the Lord
His line shall continue forever.	089. 1-2, 3-4, 26+28	Years ABC - Joseph, Husband of Mary
I believe that I shall see the good things of the Lord in the land of the living.	027. 1, 4, 7-8	Year A - Seventh Sunday of Easter
I love you, O Lord, my strength.	018. 1-2, 3+6b, 46+50ab	Year A - Thirtieth Sunday in OT
	018. 1-2, 3+6b, 46+50ab	Year B - Thirty-first Sunday in OT
I praise you, for I am wonderfully made.	139. 1-3, 13-14a, 14b-15	Years ABC - Birth of John the Baptist
I shall be satisfied, Lord, when I awake and behold your likeness.	017. 1, 5-6, 8+15	Year C - Thirty-second Sunday in OT
I shall dwell in the house of the Lord my whole life long.	023. 1-3a, 3b-4, 5, 6	Year A - Twenty-eighth Sunday in OT
I will bless your name for ever, my King and my God.	145. 1-2, 8-9, 10-11, 13cd-14	Year A - Fourteenth Sunday in OT
	145. 1-2, 8-9, 10-11, 13cd-14	Year C - Thirty-first Sunday in OT
	145. 1-2, 8-9, 10-11, 13cd-14	Years ABC - Common for OT
	145. 8-9, 10-11, 12-13	Year C - Fifth Sunday of Easter
I will extol you, Lord, for you have raised me up.	030. 1+3, 4-5, 10+11a+12b	Year B - Thirteenth Sunday in OT
	030. 1+3, 4-5, 10+11a+12b	Year C - Tenth Sunday in OT
	030. 1+3, 4-5, 10+11a+12b	Year C - Third Sunday of Easter
	030. 1+3, 4-5, 10+11a+12b	Years ABC - Easter Vigil 4
I will get up and go to my Father.	051. 1-2, 10-11, 15+17	Year C - Twenty-fourth Sunday in OT
I will lift up the cup of salvation, and call on the name of the Lord.	116. 12-13, 15-16, 17-18	Year B - Body and Blood of Christ
I will walk before the Lord, in the land of the living.	116. 1-2, 3-4, 5-6, 8-9	Year B - Twenty-fourth Sunday in OT
	116. 5-6, 10-11, 15-16	Years ABC - All Souls III
	116. 10+15, 16-17, 18-19	Year B - Second Sunday of Lent
In his days may righteousness flourish, and peace abound forever.	072. 1-2, 7-8, 12-13	Year A - Second Sunday of Advent
In you, Lord, I have found my peace.	131. 1, 2, 3	Year A - Thirty-first Sunday in OT
In your goodness, O God, you provided for the needy.	068. 3-4, 5-6a, 9-10	Year C - Twenty-second Sunday in OT
Let my tongue cling to my mouth if I do not remember you!	137. 1-2, 3-4, 5-6	Year B - Fourth Sunday of Lent
Let the light of your face shine on us, O Lord.	004. 1, 3, 6, 8	Year B - Third Sunday of Easter
Let the peoples praise you, O God, let all the peoples praise you.	067. 1-2, 4-5, 6-7	Year A - Twentieth Sunday in OT
	067. 1-2, 4-5a, 6-7	Year C - Sixth Sunday of Easter

Refrain	Psalm	Liturgical Day
May God be gracious to us and bless us.	067. 1-2, 4-5, 6-7	Years ABC - Mary, Mother of God
May the Lord bless us all the days of our lives.	128. 1-2, 3, 4-5	Year B - Twenty-seventh Sunday in OT
May the Lord come in; he is king of glory.	024. 1-2, 3-4ab, 5-6	Year A - Fourth Sunday of Advent
My God, my God, why have you forsaken me?	022. 7-8, 16-17, 18-19, 22-23	Year A - Passion Sunday
My God, my God, why have you forsaken me?	022. 7-8, 16-17, 18-19, 22-23	Year B - Passion Sunday
My God, my God, why have you forsaken me?	022. 7-8, 16-17, 18-19, 22-23	Year C - Passion Sunday
My God, my God, why have you forsaken me?	022. 7-8, 16-17, 18-19, 22-23	Years ABC - Common for Holy Week
My mouth will tell, O Lord, of your deeds of salvation.	071. 1-2, 3, 5-6, 15+17	Year C - Fourth Sunday in OT
My soul shall exult in my God.	Luke 1. 47-48, 49-50, 53-54	Year B - Third Sunday of Advent
My soul thirsts for you, O Lord my God.	063. 1, 2-3, 4-5, 7-8	Year A - Twenty-second Sunday in OT
My soul thirsts for you, O Lord my God.	063. 1, 2-3, 4-5, 6-7	Year A - Thirty-second Sunday in OT
My soul thirsts for you, O Lord my God.	063. 1, 2-3, 4-5, 7-8	Year C - Twelfth Sunday in OT
My soul thirsts for you, O Lord my God.	063. 1, 2-3, 4-5, 7-8	Years ABC - Common for OT
O bless the Lord, my soul!	104. 1b-2, 3-4, 24-25, 27+28 &c	Year C - Baptism of the Lord
O Lord, our God, how majestic is your name in all the earth!	008. 3-4, 5-6, 7-8	Year C - Trinity Sunday
O Lord, our God, you have given us the breath of life!	008. 3-4, 5-6, 7-8	Years ABC - Ext Vigil of Pentecost 1
O Lord, who may abide in your tent?	015. 1b-3a, 3b-4a, 4b-5	Year B - Twenty-second Sunday in OT
O Lord, who may abide in your tent?	015. 1b-3a, 3b-4a, 4b-5	Year C - Sixteenth Sunday in OT
O that today you would listen to the voice of the Lord. Do not harden your hearts!	095. 1-2, 6-7ab, 7c-9	Year A - Third Sunday of Lent
O that today you would listen to the voice of the Lord. Do not harden your hearts!	095. 1-2, 6-7ab, 7c-9	Year A - Twenty-third Sunday in OT
O that today you would listen to the voice of the Lord. Do not harden your hearts!	095. 1-2, 6-7ab, 7c-9	Year B - Fourth Sunday in OT
O that today you would listen to the voice of the Lord. Do not harden your hearts!	095. 1-2, 6-7ab, 7c-9	Year C - Twenty-seventh Sunday in OT
O that today you would listen to the voice of the Lord. Do not harden your hearts!	095. 1-2, 6-7ab, 7c-9	Years ABC - Common for OT
On the day I called, O Lord, you answered me.	138. 1-2a, 2b-3, 6-7ab, 7c-8	Year C - Seventeenth Sunday in OT
Our eyes look to the Lord, until he has mercy upon us.	123. 1-2a, 2b, 3-4	Year B - Fourteenth Sunday in OT
Our help is from the Lord, who made heaven and earth.	121. 1-2, 3-4, 5-6, 7-8	Year C - Twenty-ninth Sunday in OT
Praise the Lord, Jerusalem.	147. 12-13, 14-15, 19-20	Year A - Body and Blood of Christ
Praise the Lord, O my soul!	146. 6c-7, 8-9a, 9b-10	Year B - Twenty-third Sunday in OT
Praise the Lord, O my soul!	146. 6c-7, 8-9a, 9b-10	Year B - Thirty-second Sunday in OT
Praise the Lord, O my soul!	146. 6c-7, 8-9a, 9b-10	Year C - Twenty-sixth Sunday in OT
Praise the Lord who lifts up the needy.	113. 1-2, 4-6, 7-8	Year C - Twenty-fifth Sunday in OT
Proclaim the wonders of the Lord.	139. 1-3, 4+6, 7-8, 10+17	Years ABC - Ext Vigil of Pentecost 4
Protect me, O God, for in you I take refuge.	016. 5+8, 9-10, 11	Year B - Thirty-third Sunday in OT
Protect me, O God, for in you I take refuge.	016. 5+8, 9-10, 11	Years ABC - Easter Vigil 2
Restore us, O God; let your face shine, that we may be saved.	080. 1ab-2, 3-4, 14ab+18	Years ABC - Ext Vigil of Pentecost 2
Restore us, O God; let your face shine, that we may be saved.	080. 1ab+2, 14-15, 17-18	Year B - First Sunday of Advent
Restore us, O God; let your face shine, that we may be saved.	080. 1-ab+2, 14-15, 17-18	Year C - Fourth Sunday of Advent
Rise up, O Lord, and go to your resting place; you and the ark of your might.	132. 6-7, 9-10, 13-14	Years ABC - Assumption (Vigil)
Seek God in your need, and let your hearts revive.	069. 13+16, 29-30, 32-33, 35&c	Year C - Fifteenth Sunday in OT 1
Shout aloud and sing for joy: great in your midst is the Holy One of Israel.	Isaiah 12.3, 4bcd, 5-6	Year C - Third Sunday of Advent

Response	Psalm	Liturgical Day
Show us your steadfast love, O Lord, and grant us your salvation.	085. 8ab-9, 10-11, 12-13	Year A - Nineteenth Sunday in OT
	085. 8ab-9, 10-11, 12-13	Year B - Second Sunday of Advent
	085. 8ab-9, 10-11, 12-13	Year B - Fifteenth Sunday in OT
	085. 8ab-9, 10-11, 12-13	Years ABC - Common for Advent
Sing aloud to God our strength.	081. 2-3, 4-5ab, 5c-7a, 9-10ab	Year B - Ninth Sunday in OT
Sing praises to the Lord who heals the brokenhearted.	147. 1-2, 3-4, 5-6	Year B - Fifth Sunday in OT
Sing to the Lord a new song, for he has done marvellous things.	098. 1, 2-3ab, 3cd-4	Years ABC - Immaculate Conception
Taste and see that the Lord is good.	034. 1-2, 3-4, 5-6, 7-8	Year B - Nineteenth Sunday in OT
	034. 1-2, 9-10, 11-12, 13-14	Year B - Twentieth Sunday in OT
	034.1-2, 15-16, 17-18, 19-20 &c	Year B - Twenty-first Sunday in OT
	034. 1-2, 3-4, 5-6	Year C - Fourth Sunday of Lent
	034. 1-2, 3-4, 5-6, 7-8	Years ABC - Common for OT
The cup of blessing that we bless is a sharing in the Blood of Christ.	116. 12-13, 15-16, 17-18	Years ABC - Mass of the Lord's Supper
The earth is full of the steadfast love of the Lord.	033. 4-5, 6-7, 12-13, 20+22	Years ABC - Easter Vigil 1.2
The Lord gave them the bread of heaven.	078. 3+4bc, 23-24, 25-54	Year B - Eighteenth Sunday in OT
The Lord has done great things for us; we are filled with joy.	126. 1-2a, 2b-3, 4-5, 6	Year B - Thirtieth Sunday in OT
	126. 1-2a, 2b-3, 4-5, 6	Year C - Fifth Sunday of Lent
	126. 1-2a, 2b-3, 4-5, 6	Year C - Second Sunday of Advent
The Lord has established his throne in the heavens.	103. 1-2, 11-12, 19-20	Year B - Seventh Sunday of Easter
The Lord has revealed his victory in the sight of the nations.	098. 1, 2-3ab, 3cd+4	Year B - Sixth Sunday of Easter
The Lord is coming to judge the peoples with equity.	098. 1, 2-3ab, 3cd-4	Year C - Twenty-eighth Sunday in OT
	098. 5-6, 7-8, 9	Year C - Thirty-third Sunday in OT
The Lord is king; he is robed in majesty.	093. 1ab, 1c-2, 5	Year B - Christ the King
The Lord is king! Let the peoples tremble!	097. 1-2, 3-4, 5-6, 11-12	Years ABC - Ext Vigil of Pentecost 3
	097. 1-2, 6-7ac, 9+12	Year C - Seventh Sunday of Easter
The Lord is king, the most high over all the earth.	097. 1-2, 5-6, 9+12	Years ABC - Transfiguration of the Lord
The Lord is merciful and gracious.	103. 1-2, 3-4, 6-7, 8+11	Year C - Third Sunday of Lent
	103. 1-2, 3-4, 8+10, 12-13	Year A - Seventh Sunday in OT
	103. 1-2, 3-4, 8+10, 12-13	Year B - Eighth Sunday in OT
	103. 1-2, 3-4, 8+10, 12-13	Year C - Seventh Sunday in OT
	103. 1-2, 3-4, 8+10, 12-13	Years ABC - Common for OT
	103. 8+10, 13-14, 15-16, 17	Years ABC - All Souls I
The Lord is merciful and gracious; slow to anger, and abounding in steadfast love.	103. 1-2, 3-4, 9-10, 11-12	Year A - Twenty-fourth Sunday in OT
The Lord is my light and my salvation.	027. 1, 4, 13-14	Year A - Third Sunday in OT
	027. 1, 7-8, 9, 13-14	Year C - Second Sunday of Lent
	027. 1, 4, 13-14	Years ABC - Common for OT
The Lord is my shepherd; I shall not want.	023. 1-3a, 3b-4, 5, 6	Year A - Fourth Sunday of Lent
	023. 1-3a, 3b-4, 5, 6	Year A - Fourth Sunday of Easter
	023. 1-3a, 3b-4, 5, 6	Year A - Christ the King
	023. 1-3a, 3b-4, 5, 6	Year B - Sixteenth Sunday in OT
	023. 1-3a, 3b-4, 5, 6	Year C - Sacred Heart of Jesus
	023. 1-3a, 3b-4, 5, 6	Years ABC - All Souls II

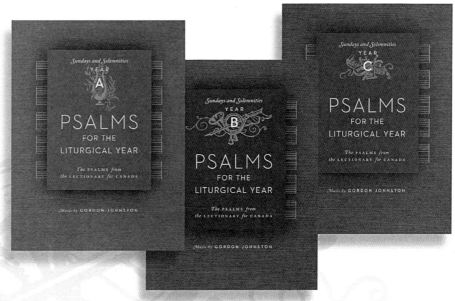

Psalms for the Liturgical Year

For Sundays and Solemnities

by Gordon Johnston

The first publication to feature psalm texts used in the new Canadian lectionary, each volume comes in a large, easy-to-use, coil-bound format and includes:

- the Psalm settings for each Sunday and all major feasts
- keyboard and guitar accompaniment
- parts for C and B-flat instruments
- a CD with MP3 files for each psalm.

To order:
Call: 1-800-387-7164 (US & Canada)
Fax: 1-800-204-4140
E-mail: books@novalis.ca

Mail a copy of this order form to:
Novalis
10 Lower Spadina Ave, Suite 400
Toronto, ON M5V 2Z2

ORDER FORM

ISBN	TITLE	QTY	PRICE	TOTAL
978-2-89646-145-5	Psalms for the Liturgical Year A		$59.95	
978-2-89646-081-6	Psalms for the Liturgical Year B		$59.95	
978-2-89646-146-2	Psalms for the Liturgical Year C		$59.95	
SAVE! Order all 3 — Product 169859			$161.87	

NOVALIS

Minimum shipping and handling: $7.00. Free shipping in Canada only for orders of $50 or more. (US and outside Canada, shipping will be charged according to method chosen. Please call for exact costs.)

GST (5%)	
SHIPPING & HANDLING	
TOTAL	

NAME	
PARISH	
MAILING ADDRESS	

CITY	PROVINCE	POSTAL CODE
PHONE NO.	FAX	EMAIL

Billing available for parish and institutional orders only. All other orders must be prepaid.
Method of Payment: ○ Cheque/Money Order enclosed   Bill my: ○ VISA ○ Mastercard

Card #   Expiry Date   /   /   Signature

This book was printed
in September 2017 by

umen l digital,
Montréal, Québec